The World's 200 Hardest

BRAIN TEASERS

The World's 200 Hardest

BRAIN TEASERS

Mind-Boggling **Puzzles**, **Problems**, and Curious **Questions** to Sharpen Your Brain

GARY R. GRUBER, PHD

Copyright © 2010 by Gary R. Gruber
Cover and internal design © 2010 by Sourcebooks, Inc.
Cover design by Larry Nozik/Nozik Design
Cover images © jfelton/iStockphoto.com, kkonkle/iStockphoto.com, tseybold/iStock photo.com, Fred-D/iStockphoto.com, emferr/iStockphoto.com

This publication is designed to provide accurate and authoritative information in regard to the subject matter covered. It is sold with the understanding that the publisher is not engaged in rendering legal, accounting, or other professional service. If legal advice or other expert assistance is required, the services of a competent professional person should be sought.—*From a Declaration of Principles Jointly Adopted by a Committee of the American Bar Association and a Committee of Publishers and Associations*

Published by Sourcebooks, Inc.
P.O. Box 4410, Naperville, Illinois 60567-4410
(630) 961-3900
Fax: (630) 961-2168
www.sourcebooks.com

Library of Congress Cataloging-in-Publication Data

Gruber, Gary R.
   The world's 200 hardest brain teasers : mind-boggling puzzles, problems, and curious questions to sharpen your brain / by Gary R. Gruber.
      p. cm.
   1. Logic puzzles. 2. Lateral thinking puzzles. 3. Word games. I. Title.
   GV1493.G77 2010
   793.73—dc22

                                    2010002994

Printed and bound in the United States of America.
VP 10 9 8 7 6 5 4 3 2 1

This book is dedicated to the thousands of people from all walks of life who have asked me to put these questions in a book and explain the answers, putting the quest for the solutions at rest.

INTRODUCTION

For years, numerous people have asked me to write this book after they were intrigued with working on these and similar problems that appeared in the various newspapers and airline magazines I write for. The problems in this book are my best and most interesting selections that will get you to think and increase your creativity. They will also help you develop your intelligence so that you will do better on all standardized tests , including the SAT, ACT, GMAT, LSAT, and GRE. Most importantly, they will give you something to look forward to and enjoy aside from your daily routine.

Many entries include an interesting anecdote about the problem and why it is so baffling, so you will get insight into a new way to think. I have also provided detailed explanations (some of which I have never before divulged) for the more difficult problems. Whatever your daily routine may be, the brain teasers in this book will challenge you to use your mind in a highly productive and rewarding way.

MY STORY

When I was in fifth grade, I had to take an IQ test. I scored 90, which is below normal and considered "dull." Although I was not told my IQ, I noticed that my teachers were not paying much attention to me and were patronizing me as if I were stupid. Later, as friends of mine were skipping grades, I was routed to the "dull classes," which embarrassed me and made me feel inferior. I felt as if I would never get far in life.

I was in seventh grade when a math teacher at my junior high school in Brooklyn, New York, told my father that he was shocked that I had only a 90 IQ. To my teacher, I seemed much smarter than that. My father was shocked to learn that I had scored a 90 on the IQ test and obtained an IQ test that was currently being administered. He gave me the test.

However, instead of actually taking it (as I had before), I started looking the test over to see what had caused me to get such a low score. This started my fascination with testing and critical thinking. I realized that certain thinking skills were being tested and that a person could actually develop those skills and hone them. I also noticed that there was a generic process to problem solving and thinking. This process was based on extracting something curious from a problem and using that to find the rest of the solution. This process provided the mechanism to think by "synthesizing" rather than just panic and rush to find an answer. As my school career unfolded, I increased my IQ to 126. I then increased the development of my thinking skills and obtained a 150.

I developed an obsession with seeing how problems can be solved. I eventually got accepted into an elite high school, and I started commenting on teachers' exams by noting on my paper, "This question could be made more interesting by adding so and so," or "This is a poor question; use this instead of that." Most of my teachers did not find this amusing (I even got detention for this behavior), but a few did—the ones who had a real interest in the learning mechanism. I started to become fascinated in how nature works, why things work the way they do, and how problems can be solved. This launched my interest in physics.

But after receiving my PhD, teaching, doing some high-powered research in physics, and even getting invited all over the world to lecture on some of the theories I developed, I realized that there was a much more serious problem to solve. There were all these young people out there who were branded like I was—dull—and were not given an opportunity to show their true talents and perhaps even genius. I felt like I was living in Thomas Gray's poem "Elegy Written in a Country Churchyard" in which he writes, "Many a flower is born to blush unseen and waste its sweet fragrance on the desert air." I realized I had a mission in life. There are all these people out there who could be great scientists, journalists, or other professionals, people who could develop their talents and become passionate about their life's work and provide us with the break-throughs we need so much. Therefore, I turned my interest and passion into the quest for how people can solve problems and learn, and how they can enjoy and develop a passion for learning and problem solving. I devoted my life to test taking, test development, critical thinking, and learning. And to my amazement I noticed, after thirty years of research, that most if not all strategies for think-ing, learning, and problem solving are based on common sense and not racking your brain.

THE GEOMETRY PROBLEM
THAT STUMPED THE NATION

Some time ago, I wrote an article titled "Are You a Genius?" that was published in newspapers all over the country. It was a twelve-question test to determine genius IQ. I received hundreds of letters from readers who could not solve the last and rather simple-looking geometry question. When I was a high school student in New York, it took me three hours to solve this problem. However, forty years later, even after being able to write thirty books on the subject of test preparation and thinking, even I could not solve the problem—and it was driving me crazy! Was I getting stupider as the years passed?

So I decided to reprint the twelve-question test, and if someone got all twelve questions right, they would be called a super genius. I was hoping someone would be able to solve the last question and then tell me how they did it. I didn't get any answers, but I did receive tons of letters asking how the twelfth problem could be geometrically solved. People at the highest levels in math at major universities, government agencies, you name it, could not solve the problem.

Then I got an urgent call on a Friday from the *Washington Post* telling me that they were getting hundreds of calls every few hours asking for a solution to the problem. I told them I could not do it. Well, that wasn't good enough for them. They said I'd better have the solution to them in four days, or else! Or else what? They couldn't sue me. For forty years I couldn't solve the problem and now I had to solve it in four days. Didn't I have better things to do over the weekend? Well, I contacted everyone I knew who was literally a genius in math, including top mathematicians in the country. I contacted fellow math students whom I hadn't talked to in thirty years, who went to school with me, and who were super math savvy and may have seen the problem. They were all eager to work on it. However, Sunday rolled around and no one responded with a solution. People from NASA, major math departments all over the country, and even the top mathematicians at Educational Testing Service (the company that develops the majority of entrance, aptitude, and achievement tests such as the SAT) could not solve the problem. In fact, one person was completely peeved, having worked 10 hours straight without a solution!

Then as a very last resort, I was able, by researching and making about twenty calls, to contact my old math professor who had given me the original problem to work on thirty years ago. But when I called him (he must have been somewhat senile), he told me that I was late for class and I'd better hand in my assignments. He kept repeating it—what a bummer! The last person on earth who could have given me the answer was incoherent! The next day I frantically called the whiz kids I went to school with who were working on the problem and asked for any hints they thought I might use. Each one of them told me to use my own specific math strategies that I have been writing about for years and using in all my test-preparation and thinking books. For example, in geometry when you want to prove that if two sides of a triangle are equal then the base angles are equal, the strategy you use is to draw a line down the triangle. This works because, almost magically, when you draw something extra, you get something for it—namely more information and an approach to the solution. I never thought about that because I thought this problem was too sophisticated! It was Monday night now and I was working feverishly on the problem using my very own strategies. The morning of the deadline came around, and I had just finished solving the problem. I told this to the *Washington Post*, and they printed a full-page solution—writing me up as "the super genius."

There are actually now six ways to solve the problem, and in this book I'll show the simplest one. See if you can figure it out. Turn to page 182 for the answer!

Given a triangle ABC, side AB = side AC. Draw a line from C to side AB. Call that line CD. Now draw a line from B to side AC. Call that line BE. Let angle EBC = 60 degrees, angle BCD = 70 degrees, angle ABE = 20 degrees, and angle DCE = 10 degrees. Now draw line DE. Find angle EDC. Do not do this trigonometrically; do it geometrically to get an exact answer.

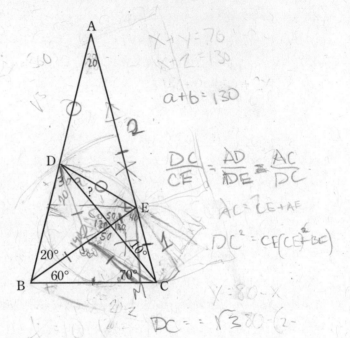

Dr. Gary R. Gruber

Note: Figures in this book are
not drawn to scale.

THE WORLD'S HARDEST BRAIN TEASERS

Here is a collection of my most interesting and mind-improving brain teasers. Many of the answers should give you a strategy for thinking, which will carry over to many other problems and provide you with thinking and problem-solving methods. There is no time limit for these questions (with exceptions as noted). Be aware that there may be more than one way to arrive at an answer to a question.

Just remember, a person who can solve problems efficiently either knows a particular strategy for the type of problem or extracts something from the problem that is curious to him or her and that leads to the next step toward a solution.

1. Two U.S. coins add up to 30 cents. If one of them is not a nickel, what are the two coins?

2. Make *one word* from all the following jumbled letters:

   o r e n o d w

3. In miles per hour, what is the average rate of a car going 20 mph and traveling back the same distance at 60 mph?
   (a) 30
   (b) 40
   (c) 50
   (d) 60
   (e) cannot be determined unless the distance is given

4. If you don't know the meaning of the word PRECURSORY, which of the following words do you think means the opposite of PRECURSORY?
    (a) flamboyant
    (b) succeeding
    (c) cautious
    (d) simple
    (e) not planned

5. An explorer found a silver coin marked 7 BC. He was told it was a forgery. Why?

    Because the calander that we use that marks 7BC wasn't around in 7BC

6. I have only nickels, dimes, and quarters and have at least one of each type of coin. The total number of coins I have is fifteen and the total value of all the coins is $1.00. How many of each coin do I have?

    35

    13 nickles   1 quarter   1 dime

7. A malicious computer program informs a user that it has "kidnapped" an important file and that what happens to the file will be based on the next statement to be typed by the user. If the user types a false statement it will delete the file, and if the user types a true statement it will change the file's name so it can never be found. The user types a statement that makes the computer unable to perform or shut down. What could the user have typed?

8. Terry is half as old as Alice was when Alice was five years older than Terry is now. How old is Terry now?

9. IMAGINARY NUMBERS is to REAL NUMBERS as
   (a) spiritual : global
   (b) infinite : finite
   (c) prime : rational
   (d) negative : positive
   (e) disordered : ordered

10. In 40 seconds or less, and without using a calculator, figure out which is greater: 354 × 357 or 355 × 356.

11. The price of a watch at a department store has been discounted 20 percent and then an additional 30 percent after the first discount was applied. Would the final discounted price have been lower if there had been a single discount of 50 percent? Why or why not?

12. A lawyer argued for $1,000,000 damages based on the following claim: His client went to an art museum, where he saw a painting of Marie Antoinette on a guillotine. He fell asleep and dreamed of the painting. At the museum's closing time, a guard tapped him on the neck just as he dreamed of the guillotine beheading Marie Antoinette. The tap provoked immediate cardiac arrest and a fatal heart attack immediately following, because he associated the tap with the guillotine blade. Why did the judge dismiss the case?

13. "Many more people who smoke develop lung cancer than those who do not smoke." What research would possibly show that cigarette smoking does not cause cancer?

14. Suppose I have 40 blue socks and 40 brown socks in a drawer. If I reach into the drawer without looking at the socks, what is the smallest amount of socks I must take out to make sure that I have a pair of socks of the same color?
    (a) 2
    (b) 3
    (c) 4
    (d) 40
    (e) 41

15. What day follows the day before yesterday if two days from now will be Sunday?

16. MUSIC : VIOLIN ::

    (a) notes : composer

    (b) sound : musical instrument

    (c) crayon : drawing

    (d) furniture : carpentry tools

    (e) symphony : piano

17. What is the next number in the following sequence:

    0 0 1 2 2 4 3 6 4 8 5 ?

    (a) 6

    (b) 8

    (c) 10

    (d) 12

    (e) 14

18. GEORGE WASHINGTON : CHERRY TREE ::

(a) Jonas Salk : polio vaccine

(b) Abraham Lincoln : emancipation

(c) Thomas Edison : lightbulb

(d) Thomas Jefferson : constitution

(e) John Hancock : signature

19. A triangle has sides of lengths A, B, and C. Which is true?

(a) C minus B is always greater than A

(b) C minus B is always less than A

(c) C minus B is always equal to A

(d) None of the above comparisons can be made between
     C minus B and A.

20. The following characteristics apply to a group of people in a room: Fourteen are blonds, eight are blue-eyed, and two are neither blond nor blue-eyed. If five of the people are blue-eyed blonds, how many people are in the room?

    (a) 3

    (b) 17

    (c) 19

    (d) 24

    (e) 29

21. Suppose you have a 12-hour digital clock where the number representing the hour is always the same as the number representing the minute. That is, the clock can only show times like 8:08, 9:09, 10:10, etc. What is the smallest time difference between two such times?

    (a) 101 minutes

    (b) 61 minutes

    (c) 60 minutes

    (d) 49 minutes

    (e) 11 minutes

22. A square, ABCD, is inscribed in a quarter-circle where B is on the circumference of the circle and D is the center of the circle. What is the length of diagonal AC of the square if the circle's radius is 5?

   (a) 3

   (b) 4

   (c) 5

   (d) 6

   (e) The length cannot be determined.

23. 50 × 50 × 50 ×...(where there are a hundred 50s) is how many times 100 × 100 × 100 ×...(where there are fifty 100s)?

   (a) 25 × 25 × 25 ×...(where there are fifty 25s)

   (b) 4 × 4 × 4 ×...(where there are fifty 4s)

   (c) 2 × 2 × 2 ×...(where there are fifty 2s)

   (d) 1 time

   (e) None of these answers is correct.

24. How could you figure out the meaning of the word INEXTRICABLE?

25. A doctor's son's father was not a doctor. How is this possible?

26. What's wrong with this advertisement: "Shop early and avoid the crowds."

27. You are competing in a linear race and overtake the runner in second place.

In which position are you now?

(a) first
(b) second
(c) third
(d) fourth
(e) cannot be determined

28. Bonnie's father has five daughters but has no sons. Four of the daughters are named Chacha, Cheche, Chichi, and Chocho. What is the fifth daughter's name?

(a) Chuchu

(b) Chochu

(c) Chuchy

(d) Chochy

(e) none of the above

29. HELMET : HEAD ::

(a) sword : warrior

(b) umbrella : clothing

(c) shoe : sock

(d) watch : wrist

(e) thimble : finger

30. Suppose a four-digit number is an exact multiple of 9 and three of the four digits are 1, 2, and 3. What is the fourth digit?

31. A knight wants to marry a princess and she wants to marry him. However, the king demands that the knight draw one of two slips of paper from a box. The king says one will say "Death" and the other "Marriage." The princess whispers to her suitor that both slips say "Death." What could the knight do to wed the princess?

32. There are four people in a line. Sarah is between Barry and Mary. Mary is in front of two other people, and John is directly in front of Mary. Who's first in line, second, third, and fourth?

33. Which is greater, one-half the surface area of a ball with radius 3″ or the area of a circle with radius 3″?

34. In the following subtraction problem, each letter uniquely represents one digit from 0 to 9. At least one digit is not 0. Find the values of A, B, and C.

```
  A B A
-   C A
  -----
    A B
```

35. What is the next letter in the following series: y z v w s t p q ?
    (a) l
    (b) m
    (c) n
    (d) o
    (e) p

36. What is the value of x in the diagram below?

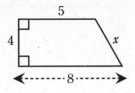

37. If A = 250 percent of B, what percent of A is B?
    (a) 1/250 percent
    (b) 25 percent
    (c) 40 percent
    (d) 50 percent
    (e) 125 percent

38. Suppose a car goes uphill a certain distance at the rate of A miles per hour. Then the car travels downhill the same distance at a rate of B miles per hour. Which is greater, the average of the rates A and B, or the average rate of the car for the whole trip (uphill and downhill)? Assume that the value of A is not the same as the value of B.

39. Put these statements in the right order:

(a) The ship stopped to anchor in Commander Bay.

(b) A boy awoke and saw a sea lion.

(c) A boy went ashore and napped in a meadow.

(d) A boy did not tell what he had seen.

(e) A boy got a job on a ship.

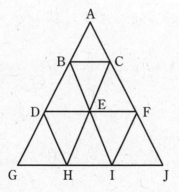

40. How many triangles are there in the figure above?

(a) 9

(b) 10

(c) 11

(d) 12

(e) 13

(f) none of the above

41. Suppose a bird is standing in a closed box that is resting on a scale. When the bird flies in the box, does the scale read the same as, more than, or less than when the bird is resting?

42. You are competing in a linear race and overtake the last runner. In which position are you now?
    (a) last
    (b) second to last
    (c) third to last
    (d) cannot be determined unless the number of runners is known
    (e) cannot be determined because this is an ambiguous question

43. In 20 seconds or less, determine which is greater:
    (a) 410/963 – 208/962
    (b) 202/962

44. MOTH : CLOTHING ::
    (a) sheep : wool
    (b) butterfly : wood
    (c) puncture : tire
    (d) tear : sweater
    (e) termite : house

45. Assuming the statement "Only the good die young," is true, we
    can infer which two of the following?
    (a) No good person lives to an old age.
    (b) Anyone who lives to an old age must be bad.
    (c) Only bad people do not die young.
    (d) All bad people do not die young.
    (e) Some bad people die young.

46. Harry owes Sam $30. Sam owes Phil $20. Phil owes Harry $50. Which of the following will settle the debts?

    (a) Harry could give Phil $50.

    (b) Sam could give Phil $20 and Harry could give Sam $40.

    (c) Harry could give Phil $20 and Sam could give Phil $10.

    (d) Sam and Phil could give Harry $50 total.

    (e) Phil could give Harry $20 and could give Sam $10.

47. If nobody loves nobody, which of the following must be true?

    I. Everybody loves somebody.

    II. Somebody loves somebody.

    III. Nobody loves anybody.

    (a) I only

    (b) II only

    (c) III only

    (d) I and II only

    (e) II and III only

48. Solve this in thirty seconds or less: The following are dimensions of five rectangular boxes. Which box has a volume different from the other four?
    (a) $5 \times 8 \times 12$
    (b) $15 \times 16 \times 2$
    (c) $3 \times 32 \times 5$
    (d) $3 \times 4 \times 40$
    (e) $2 \times 6 \times 36$

49. A clothing store offers successive discounts of 30 percent and 10 percent on a sweater. The equivalent single discount would be:
    (a) 34 percent
    (b) 36 percent
    (c) 37 percent
    (d) 38 percent
    (e) 40 percent

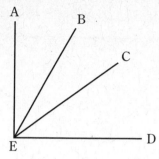

50. Shown above, angle AED = 90°, angle BED = 40°, and angle AEC = 75°. What is the measure of angle BEC?

51. In ten seconds and without a calculator, determine whether 999 × 1,001 is greater than, less than, or equal to 1,000 × 1,000.

52. If there are twenty-four people at a party and each person shakes another person's hand, how many handshakes are there?

53. Which verb does not belong with the others in this set?

BRING BUY CATCH DRAW FIGHT SEEK TEACH THINK

54. The three symbols in sets I and II have something in common. What must the last symbol be so that an analogy exists between the first and second set?

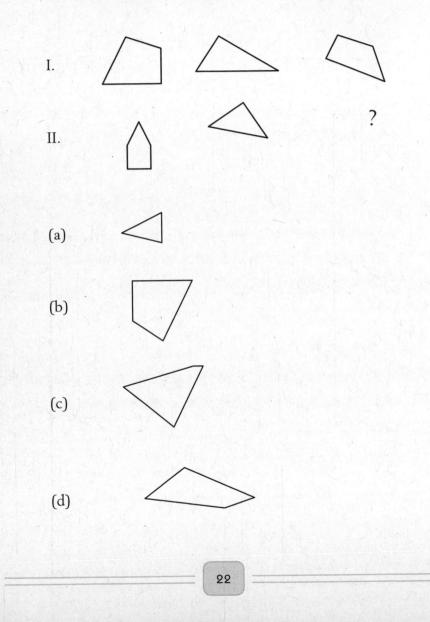

I.

II.

?

(a)

(b)

(c)

(d)

55. What three letters can be jumbled to make at least 3 three-letter words using the three letters?

56. What is the three-digit number that can be made from the digits 2, 3, 5, and 7 where no two digits in the three-digit number are alike, and where the three-digit number is a multiple of each of the digits chosen?

57. What six-letter English word can be produced from a three-letter abbreviation for one month followed by a three-letter abbreviation for another month?

58. ABCD is a parallelogram (AB is parallel to DC, and AD is parallel to BC). A perpendicular line is drawn from A to DC, of length h, and angle D is 60°.

    Which is greater: $h \times AB$ or $AD \times CD$?

59. At noon and at midnight, the long and short hands of a clock are together. Between noon and midnight, how many times does the long hand pass the short hand?

60. Find a word that has the same meaning when a prefix is placed before the word.

61. Given a triangle ABC, draw the altitude BD to side AC and draw the altitude CE to side AB. If AC is greater than AB, what can you say about the relationship between the length of BD and CE? That is, is BD greater than CE, less than CE, or equal to CE?

62. Anne has three blouses, four skirts, and two pairs of shoes. How many different outfits can she wear if an outfit consists of any blouse worn with any skirt and either pair of shoes?

63. Take 1,000. Add 40. Add another 1,000. Add 30. Add 1,000 again. Add 20. Add 1,000. And add 10. What is the total?

    (a) 5,000

    (b) 4,900

    (c) 4,100

    (d) 4,000

    (e) none of the above

64. What is the next letter in the following sequence: a b d g k ?

    (a) m

    (b) n

    (c) o

    (d) p

    (e) q

65. How many positive integers between 0 and 1000 are <u>not</u> exactly divisible by 3?

66. What's the answer when you divide 40 by 1/2 and add 20?

67. TURTLE : REPTILE ::
    (a) oak : tree
    (b) leaf : branch
    (c) trout : fish
    (d) snake : rattle
    (e) oyster : clam

68. Name six English five-letter words that also make an English word when a letter is placed in front of the word.

69. Put these statements in the right order:
    (a) A woman tries on a dress.
    (b) A woman buys a hat.
    (c) A man buys a dress.
    (d) A woman returns a dress to a store.
    (e) A man gives his wife a present.

70. The three letters in sets I and II have something in common. What letter should "?" be so that an analogy exists between the first and second set?

I. A E L

II. P Q ?

(a) M

(b) T

(c) U

(d) V

(e) W

71. The sum of two whole positive (greater than 0) numbers is 3. One of them is not 2. What is one of the numbers?

(a) 0

(b) 2

(c) 3

(d) 4

(e) cannot be determined

72. What is the length of line x in the diagram? (Note: Diagram is not drawn to scale.)

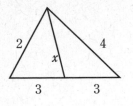

73. A test was taken by 60 students and was scored on a scale from 0 to 100. Only 21 students scored higher than or equal to 80. What is the smallest possible average score of all 60 students?

74. What is maximum number of boxes 9 inches × 6 inches × 3 inches that will fit into a closet that measures 6 feet × 4 feet × 2.5 feet?

75. Can you solve this in five seconds?

    Which is greater, 3/7 or 7/16?

76. In ten seconds or less, express 1,111 divided by 25 as a percent.

77. Using root meanings to help you, define the meaning of the word MANUMIT.
    (a) to manufacture
    (b) to be masculine
    (c) to set free

78. What is the next letter in the following sequence: a z c w e t g q i?
    (a) n
    (b) k
    (c) l
    (d) m
    (e) o

79. How many different committees can be formed from a pool of three people, where a committee can consist of one to three people?

    (a) 3
    (b) 4
    (c) 5
    (d) 6
    (e) 7

80. Which of the following fractions is smallest?

    (a) 11/20
    (b) 5/6
    (c) 5/7
    (d) 2/3
    (e) 3/4

81. If a, b, and c are consecutive odd integers whose sum is 57, what is c?

82. A man with a number of bookshelves has distributed his book collection evenly on the shelves, putting 80 books on each shelf. If he adds 3 shelves and redistributes his collection evenly on all the shelves, each shelf will have 50 books. How many books are in his collection?

83. A sundial is the type of timepiece that has the fewest moving parts. What type of timepiece has the most moving parts?

84. Suppose you have a strainer whose measurements are 4″ wide × 3″ high × 6″ long. How much water can it hold?

85. In 10 seconds, without multiplying 35 × 65 and 34 × 66, determine which is greater: 35 × 65 or 34 × 66.

86. Choose any two-digit number. Add the digits. Then subtract that result from the original number to get a final result. Which of the following numbers could be your final result?
    (a) 31
    (b) 32
    (c) 33
    (d) 34
    (e) 35
    (f) 36

87. Name three words that end in "DOUS."

88. Rearranging the letters MEANYRG would give you the name of:
    (a) an animal
    (b) a state
    (c) a city
    (d) an ocean
    (e) a country

89. Three messages were received from Mars.
    1. "Avion Balcon Sondor," which was translated to "Serious Spaceship Fumes."
    2. "Mayar Pulgar Avion," which was translated to "Serious Atmosphere Particles."
    3. "Balcon Roctos Vivand," which was translated to "Dangerous Liquid Fumes."

    What would the word SONDOR mean?

    (a) Liquid
    (b) Fumes
    (c) Atmosphere
    (d) Spaceship
    (e) Particles

90. If everyone working at a car wash works at the same speed, and eight people can wash 50 cars in 60 hours, then four people can wash 100 cars in how many hours?
    (a) 30
    (b) 60
    (c) 120
    (d) 240
    (e) 360

91. If some Blips are Plips and some Plips are Jips, then "some Blips are Jips"
    (a) is true
    (b) is false
    (c) cannot be determined as true or false

92. Matt is the fiftieth fastest and the fiftieth slowest runner in his school. Assuming no two runners are the same speed, how many runners are in Matt's school?
    (a) 50
    (b) 51
    (c) 99
    (d) 100
    (e) 101

93. Peter is taller than Nancy and Dan is shorter than Peter. Which of the following can be proved true:
    (a) Dan is taller than Nancy.
    (b) Dan is shorter than Nancy.
    (c) Dan is as tall as Nancy.
    (d) None of the above can be proved true.

94. Together Harry and Sam caught 32 fish. Harry caught three times as many fish as Sam. How many fish did Harry catch?

    (a) 6

    (b) 8

    (c) 16

    (d) 24

    (e) 28

95. Two runners start at the same point facing in opposite directions. Each runner then runs 3 straight miles, takes a right turn, and runs straight for another 4 miles. What is the distance in miles between the two runners at that point?

    (a) 5

    (b) 8

    (c) 10

    (d) 12

    (e) 14

96. What is the shortest name of a U.S. state that shares a letter in common with each of the other fifty states?

97. How many ways can four people be seated at one table for four, with two people facing the other two people?

98. Is it possible for a man in California to marry his widow's sister?

99. A farmer has 17 sheep and all but 9 die. How many are left?

100. Refrigerators come in cartons 40 inches deep × 48 inches wide × 60 inches high. They must stand upright when stored. If Jones has a storage room 45 feet across, 60 feet deep, and 8 feet high, what is the greatest number of refrigerators he can store there?
    (a) 180
    (b) 195
    (c) 198
    (d) 201
    (e) 396

101. Which is greater, Quantity A or Quantity B? Or are they equal?

QUANTITY A: The average rate of a car traveling uphill at a rate of a miles an hour and downhill the same distance at a rate of b miles an hour.

QUANTITY B: The average of the rates of a miles an hour and b miles an hour.

102. What can we infer from the following statement?

"Since every child I know likes ice cream, Mike must also like ice cream."

(a) The speaker doesn't know many children.
(b) Mike is a child.
(c) Mike likes anything sweet.
(d) The speaker is a good friend of Mike's.
(e) The speaker saw Mike eat ice cream.

103. What word would become smaller when you add additional letters?

104. Do they have a fourth of July in England?

105. How many birthdays does the average man have?

106. How many outs are there in an inning?

107. A clerk in the butcher shop is 5′10″ tall. What does he weigh?

108. The three symbols in sets I and II have something in common. What must the "?" be so that an analogy exists between the first and second set?

Set I:

Set II: ?

(a)

(b)

(c)

(d)

(e)

109. How many two-cent stamps are there in a dozen?

110. If a doctor gives you three pills, telling you to take one every half hour, how many minutes will pass from taking the first pill to the last pill?

111. One of the numbers between 3,000 and 4,000 with digits increasing from left to right is 3,457. How many different numbers are there with digits that increase from left to right between 4,000 and 5,000?

112. What is the next number in the following sequence: 125, 64, 27, 8?

113. John is 10 years old, and his mother is four times as old as he is. When John is 15 years old, how old will his mother be? (Assuming she is not dead.)

(a) 65

(b) 60

(c) 55

(d) 50

(e) 45

114. Suppose a car goes uphill a distance of 1 mile, then immediately turns around and goes downhill the same distance, and suppose the average rate of the car for the whole trip is 20 miles per hour. What is the total time spent going uphill and downhill in minutes?

(a) 6

(b) 8

(c) 10

(d) cannot be determined unless the time going downhill is given

(e) cannot be determined unless the speed going uphill is given

115. If you are in an elevator stopped on the thirty-ninth floor of a hotel and the cable breaks and no help is available, what do you do to save yourself?

     (a) Just before the elevator hits the ground, you jump up.
     (b) Hold on to anything and stay still.
     (c) Lie down flat in the elevator.
     (d) You can't do anything.

116. Is 46 × 767 × 72 greater, less than, or equal to 767 × 46 × 74? You have three seconds to answer.

117. Create a sentence such that when "which" is replaced by "that" and the commas are inserted in the appropriate places, the sentence has a different meaning.

118. Nine people are on a straight line inside a circle. What is the least number of people that must move from the line in order for all nine people to be on the circumference of the circle?

119. In five seconds or less, which is greater: 1 or 77/99 divided by 99/77?

120. Fill in the blanks to complete the sentence: While a television course is not able to _____ a live course, it is still able to teach the _____ aspects of the subject.
    (a) develop...necessary
    (b) replace...important
    (c) manage...relevant
    (d) create...negative
    (e) anticipate...inconsequential

121. What is the main problem with the following argument? "Women are better than men in tennis. It is true that Bobby (Robert) Riggs beat Margaret Court, but he played like a woman and she played like a man."

122. VACCINATION : DISEASE ::
     (a) aspirin : headache
     (b) studying : learning
     (c) physician : patient
     (d) trial : judgment
     (e) freezing : spoilage

123. Mary must get up at 7 AM to get to work on time. Her clock gains 9 minutes every 3 days. If she sets it correctly at 11 PM on Sunday night, at what time should she get up, according to her clock, on Tuesday morning?

124. Phil is taking a 100-mile trip. If he averages 25 miles per hour during the first 50 miles, what must he average during the second 50 miles to make his average speed for the whole trip 50 miles per hour?

125. There are nine coins that are identical in appearance. One weighs more than the others, which have equal weight. With a balance scale to determine the coin that is heavier in only two weighings, how many coins on each side of the balance scale would you weigh first?

(a) 1 vs. 1

(b) 2 vs. 2

(c) 3 vs. 3

(d) 4 vs. 4

(e) none of these

126. One segment of the game show *Let's Make a Deal* had three doors—behind one door was a new car and behind each of the other two was a goat. The contestant would win whatever was behind the door he or she chose. The contestant chose one of the three doors, but before it was opened, the host opened up a different door that had a goat behind it. In order to have the greatest chance of winning the car, should the contestant open the door that was his or her original choice or open the remaining door?

127. The following words were in a sentence in the following sequence: XYere ZYere Xere. What letters do X, Y, and Z represent?

128. Suppose you can purchase donuts in boxes of 6, 9, and 20. What is the greatest number of donuts you cannot purchase?

129. In 10 seconds, with or without a calculator, what is the value of $2/3 \times 3/4 \times 4/5 \times 5/6 \times 6/7$?

130. LIAR : MENDACIOUS ::
     (a) disease : toxic
     (b) artist : creative
     (c) conductor : symphonic
     (d) pygmy : undersized
     (e) fib : concerned

131. What is the next letter in the following series: a l b e m f i n j ?
     (a) l
     (b) m
     (c) o
     (d) p
     (e) q

132. Suppose you have three Scrabble tiles: N, T, and O. What is the probability that when you randomly place the three tiles upright in a row, they spell an English word?

133. What is the value of the sum of the first 99 consecutive integers? (In other words, what is 1 + 2 + 3 + 4 +...+ 99?)

134. Suppose we have the sequence (1), (2,3), (4,5,6), (7,8,9,10), (11,12,13,14,15)...where (1) is the first part of the sequence (2,3) the second part, etc. What is the first number of the 100th part of the sequence?

135. In an isosceles triangle, ABC, AB = AC, and angle A = 20°. Point P is on side AC such that AP = BC. Find angle PBC.

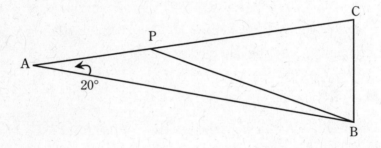

136. P is a point inside a square ABCD such that PA = 1, PB = 2, and PC = 3. What is the measure of angle APB?

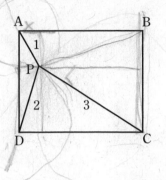

137. Which two words do not belong with the others?

(a) fallible

(b) congruous

(c) flammable

(d) famous

(e) exact

138.

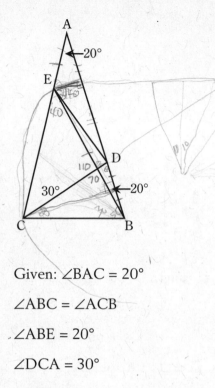

Given: ∠BAC = 20°

∠ABC = ∠ACB

∠ABE = 20°

∠DCA = 30°

∠BED = ?

And do it without trigonometry!

139. I throw a five-cent coin and a ten-cent coin in the air. If one of them lands as a head, what is the probability that the five-cent coin will land as a head?

(a) 1/3

(b) 1/2

(c) 2/3

(d) 3/4

(e) 7/8

140. Three items in a department store are sold with successive discounts.

The first is sold with successive discounts of 60 percent and 40 percent.

The second is sold with successive discounts of 50 percent and 50 percent.

And the third is sold with successive discounts of 30 percent and 70 percent.

Which of the following is true:
(a) The equivalent single discount of all three items is the same, but not 100 percent.
(b) The equivalent discount of each of the three items is between 70 percent and 80 percent.
(c) The equivalent discount of each of the three items is between 80 percent and 90 percent.
(d) The equivalent discount of each of the three items is 100 percent.
(e) None of the above statements is true.

141. You have an empty three-gallon bottle and an empty five-gallon bottle. How can you measure exactly one gallon of milk without wasting any milk?

142. You have three playing cards lying face up, side by side. A five is just to the right of a two. A five is just to the left of a two. A spade is just to the left of a club, and a spade is just to the right of a spade. What are two possible layouts for the three cards?

143. If the following four statements are presented, which one of them is true?
(a) The number of false statements here is one.
(b) The number of false statements here is two.
(c) The number of false statements here is three.
(d) The number of false statements here is four.

144. Find a four-digit number where the first digit is one-third the second, the third is the sum of the first and second, and the last is three times the second.

145. A boy and a girl are sitting on a bench. "I'm a girl," says the child with brown hair. "I'm a boy," says the child with blond hair. If at least one of them is lying, which one is lying, or are they both lying?

146. You have twelve balls that are identical in all ways, except one ball is heavier than the rest. With a balance scale, how could you determine in three weighings which is the heavy ball?

147. If you add the age of a man to the age of his wife, the result is 91. He is now twice as old as she was when he was as old as she is now. How old is the man and how old is his wife?

148. Suppose you have fifty American coins with at least one quarter, totaling exactly $1.00. If you drop a coin at random, what is the probability that it is a penny?

149. Bill bought four times as many apples as Harry, and this amount happened to be three times as many as Martin bought. If Bill, Harry, and Martin purchased a total of less than 190 apples, what is the greatest number of apples that Bill could have purchased?

(a) 168
(b) 120
(c) 119
(d) 117
(e) 108
(f) 90

150. Put the numbers 1 through 9 in the circles below so that the numbers in four circles on each side add up to 17. Note: You can't use a number more than once.

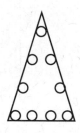

151. Using six straight lines without retracing, connect all sixteen circles.

O O O O

O O O O

O O O O

O O O O

152. Suppose there are two buckets, one that contains a gallon of water and the other that contains a gallon of alcohol. A cup of alcohol from the second bucket is poured into the bucket of water. A cup of the resulting mixture is then poured back into the bucket of alcohol. Which is now true?

(a) There is more water in the alcohol than alcohol in the water.

(b) There is more alcohol in the water than water in the alcohol.

(c) There is the same amount of water in the alcohol as alcohol in the water.

153. A figure is divided into two squares by drawing one straight line.
The original figure could have been a/an:
(a) nonrectangular trapezoid
(b) triangle
(c) square
(d) circle
(e) octagon

154. What is the next letter in the following series: s t n o j k g h ?
(a) g
(b) c
(c) d
(d) e
(e) f

155. A bus can hold x people. It is half full, and y people now get off.
How many people could now get on the bus?

156. Unscramble the words to make a phrase about the movies:

    SGITHL, AEMRAC, CTONIA

157. If I have 3 dimes, 3 nickels and 3 quarters, how many ways can I make change for $1.00?
    (a) 1
    (b) 2
    (c) 3
    (d) 4
    (e) 5

158. Three friends eat breakfast at a restaurant. They estimate that the bill should come to $30. They split the bill 3 ways and pay $10 each. When the bill comes, it is $25. Since this is not divisible by 3, they each take $1 back, and a $2 tip is left. Since each paid $9 and $9 × 3 = $27, plus $2 for the tip, where did the extra dollar go?

159. What is the least whole number greater than 95,555 where four of the digits of the number are the same?

160. What English word contains all the vowels, in alphabetical order?

161. How many states are there in the United States where the first letter of the capital city is the same as the first letter of the state?

162. BUILDING : CHURCH ::
   (a) dance : ballet
   (b) poetry : sonnet
   (c) museum : relics
   (d) song : hymn
   (e) morality : ethics

163. HAMLET : VILLAGE ::
     (a) street : sidewalk
     (b) highway : car
     (c) building : skyscraper
     (d) photograph : portrait
     (e) cottage : house

164. Fill in the blanks:

    In spite of the _____ of her presentation, many people were
    _____ with the speaker's concepts and ideas.

    (a) interest…enthralled
    (b) power…taken
    (c) intensity…shocked
    (d) greatness…gratified
    (e) strength…bored

165. Fill in the blank:

Richard Wagner was frequently intolerant; moreover, his strange behavior caused most of his acquaintances to _____ the composer whenever possible.

(a) contradict
(b) interrogate
(c) shun
(d) revere
(e) tolerate

Read the following passage and answer the questions that follow:

Sometimes the meaning of glowing water is ominous. Off the Pacific coast of North America, it may mean that the sea is filled with a minute plant that contains a poison of strange and terrible virulence. About four days after this minute plant comes to dominate the coastal plankton, some of the fishes and shellfish in the vicinity become toxic. This is because in their normal feeding, they have strained the poisonous plankton out of the water.

166. Fish and shellfish become toxic when they:
    (a) swim in poisonous water
    (b) feed on poisonous plants
    (c) change their feeding habits
    (d) give off a strange glow
    (e) take strychnine into their system

167. If there was a paragraph preceding the one in the passage, it most probably discussed:
    (a) phenomena of the Pacific coastline
    (b) poisons that affect man
    (c) toxic plants in the sea
    (d) characteristics of plankton
    (e) phenomena of the sea

168. A four-sided figure, ABCD, contains interior right angle C. AB = 12, BC = 3, CD = 4, and AD = 13. What is the area of the figure ABCD?

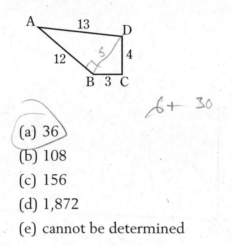

6+ 30

(a) 36

(b) 108

(c) 156

(d) 1,872

(e) cannot be determined

169. If x + y = 7 and xy = 4, then find the value of (x × x) + (y × y). Note: x and y may not be integers.

170. A four-sided figure has sides of lengths *a*, *b*, *c*, and *d*. Sides of lengths *c* and *d* meet at a right angle (90°). Sides of lengths *a* and *d* meet at a 140° angle. Sides of lengths *b* and *c* meet at a 40° angle. Is $a^2 - c^2$ greater than, equal to, or less than $d^2 - b^2$?

171. If *a* does not equal *b* and *a* + *b* is greater than 0, is 2*ab* divided by (*a* + *b*) greater than, equal to, or less than (*a* + *b*) divided by 2?

172. Fill in the blanks:

His choice for the new judge won the immediate _____ of city officials, even though some of them had _____ about him.

(a) acclaim…reservations
(b) disdain…information
(c) apprehension…dilemmas
(d) vituperation…repercussions
(e) enmity…preconceptions

173. SHIP : HARBOR ::
(a) flower : garden
(b) village : people
(c) nest : bird
(d) editor : newspaper
(e) car : garage

174. In the diagram, where a circle is inscribed in a square and another square is inscribed in the circle, if a side of the larger
square is 10, what is the area of the smaller square?

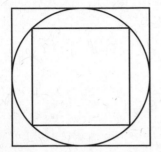

175. What is the opposite of EBULLIENT?
    (a) aggressive
    (b) tranquil
    (c) compliant

176. How many integers between 10 and 100 are divisible by 3?

177. The volume of a cube is 27. What is the sum of the length of all its edges?

178. What is the next letter in the following series:

    a c d b e g h i f j l m n ?

    (a) k
    (b) l
    (c) m
    (d) n
    (e) o

179. It takes Jim 4 hours to do a job. It takes Tom 2 hours to do the same job. How many such jobs could they do together in 4 hours?

180. A survey of 50 people who can write showed that 20 could write only with their left hand and 10 could write with either hand. How many could write with their right hand?

    (a) 30

    (b) 20

    (c) 25

    (d) 10

    (e) 40

181. The average of the number 10 and some unknown number, x, is divided by the sum of 10 and x. The result is 1/2. What is the value of x?

182. The difference between the greatest and smallest two-digit even integers that are exactly divisible by 4 is:

    (a) 82

    (b) 84

    (c) 96

    (d) 88

    (e) 80

183. How far would a bicycle wheel of diameter 2 feet roll in 700 revolutions?

184. A typist increased her speed from 60 words per minute to 80 words per minute. What percent did her speed increase?

185. If a sheet of cardboard has an area of 186 square inches, and two pieces each measuring 6 inches × 3 inches are cut out, what is the area of the remaining cardboard?

186. Put the following statements in the correct order:
(a) The price of gasoline doubles.
(b) A man cancels an order for a car.
(c) A man's car is totally demolished in an accident.
(d) A man orders a compact car.
(e) A man orders a high horsepower car.

187. COURT : LITIGATION ::
     (a) settlement : client
     (b) prayer : litany
     (c) judge : lawyer
     (d) reconciliation : dispute
     (e) tournament : joust

188. A certain orchestra has exactly three times as many string mu-
     sicians as musicians playing wind instruments. Which of the
     following can be the combined number of string and wind musi-
     cians in this orchestra?
     (a) 27
     (b) 28
     (c) 29
     (d) 30
     (e) 31

189. OBOE : BASSOON ::
    (a) viola : cello
    (b) trumpet : violin
    (c) mountain : peak
    (d) globe : city
    (e) antonym : pseudonym

190. Carl has four times as many quarters as Steve and three times as many quarters as William. If Carl, Steve, and William have a total of less than 200 quarters, what is the greatest number of quarters that Carl could have?

191. Jane is three times as old as Ann; three years ago, Ann was a year younger than Joyce is now. If Ellen is twice as old as Ann, list the four girls in descending age order.

192. A girl has exactly enough money to buy three sweaters and two skirts, or three skirts and no sweaters. All sweaters are the same price, and all skirts are the same price. What is the maximum number of sweaters she can buy if she buys only one skirt?

193. Beads are strung onto a necklace in this order: red, white, green. A design that begins on red and ends on white could be composed of the following number of beads:

I. 17

II. 29

III. 35

(a) I only

(b) III only

(c) II and III only

(d) I and III only

(e) I, II, and III

194. Put the following statements in the correct order:

    (a) A student buys a bicycle.

    (b) A student rides to school on the subway.

    (c) A student leaves for school at 8:00 AM.

    (d) A student leaves for school at 8:30 AM.

    (e) The price of a subway fare doubles.

195. LULLABY : CRADLE ::

    (a) birth : marriage

    (b) barcarole : gondola

    (c) song : poem

    (d) carol : sonneteer

    (e) night : morning

196. It is not true that both Freddie and Susan will be hired by Phoenix labs. Which of the following is possible based on the previous statement?

I Either Freddie or Susan will be hired by Phoenix labs.

II Neither Freddie nor Susan will be hired by Phoenix labs.

III Freddie and Susan will be hired by Phoenix labs.

IV Freddie will be hired by Phoenix labs only if Susan is.

V Either Freddie or Susan will not be hired by Phoenix labs.

(a) I only

(b) II only

(c) III only

(d) IV only

(e) V only

(f) I, II, and V only

197. The perimeter of this figure is:

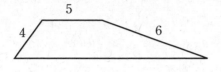

(a) a whole number
(b) less than 30
(c) greater than 40
(d) 22
(e) 20

198. Which fraction is greater, or are they equal?

The area of a circle circumscribed about a square
_____
The area of the circle inscribed in the same square

OR

The area of a square circumscribed about a circle
_____
The area of the square inscribed in the same circle

199. A soldier has been captured by the enemy. He is so brave that they offer to let him choose how he wants to be killed. They tell him, "If you tell a lie you will be shot, and if you tell the truth you will be hanged." He can only make one statement. He makes a statement and goes free. What could he have said?

(a) "I will be hanged."

(b) "I will be shot."

(c) "I will not be shot or be hanged."

(d) "I will be shot or be hanged."

(e) "I am not a liar."

200. On a street there are 25 houses—10 of the houses have fewer than six rooms, 10 of the houses have more than seven rooms, and 4 houses have more than eight rooms. What is the total number of houses that are either six, seven, or eight rooms?

(a) 5

(b) 9

(c) 11

(d) 14

(e) 15

201. Name twenty English four-letter words that also make an English word when a letter is placed in front of the word.

202. What do these numbers have in common?

     111, 112, 115, 128, 132, 135, 144, 175, 212, 216, 224, 312, 315, 384, 432, 612, 624, 672, 735, 816

203. A horse is pulling a cart. It is a known fact that the force that the horse exerts on the cart is equally balanced by the force that the cart exerts on the horse (Newton's third law). Since both of these forces balance (net "0"), how do the horse and cart move?

204. What is the largest number one can write using only four 4s?

205. What percent of 5 is 20? (65 percent of California students got the answer to this question wrong!)

    (a) 25
    (b) 40
    (c) 100
    (d) 200
    (e) 400

206. A rectangle is inscribed in a quarter-circle as shown below The radius of the circle is 5 inches. Find the length of the diagonal of the rectangle as shown in the diagram.

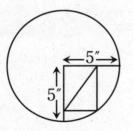

207. This problem had baffled three Physics Nobel Prize winners—and it doesn't seem that hard!

Note: This question is much more difficult than problem 146, where you know that the "odd" ball is heavier than the rest.

Twelve balls are identical in all ways except one has a different weight. Three weighings on a balance scale will not only identify the odd ball, but also tell whether it is heavier or lighter. How many balls must be put on each side of the scale in the first weighing, the second weighing, and the third weighing?

Answer should be in this form (this is only a sample answer, not necessarily the correct one):

First weighing—six against six

Second weighing—three against three

Third weighing—one against one

208. On the *Tonight Show with Johnny Carson,* Carson spent fifteen minutes trying to solve this problem and no one, including himself, could do it!

A teacher shows three very bright students three red hats and two white ones. The students are then blindfolded and the teacher puts one hat on each of their heads and the remaining hats in a closed bag. The first student removes his blindfold and is able only to see the other two students' hats. He says he cannot say for certain the color of his own hat.

After hearing the first student, the second student removes her blindfold, sees the other two students' hats, and says that she cannot say for certain the color of her own hat. After thinking and without removing his blindfold, the last student says he knows the color of his hat. Which is false? Note: Any combination of a, b, c, d, and e may be the correct answer.

(a) The third student has enough information to determine the color of his hat without removing his blindfold.

(b) The third student's hat can be white.

(c) The three students' hats can be the same color.

(d) Both remaining hats in the bag can be red.

(e) There are exactly four possible combinations of hat colors on the students' heads.

209. This can be a real brain racker unless you know some important math strategies.

     A ship is twice as old as the ship's boiler was when the ship was as old as the boiler is. The ratio of the boiler's age now to the ship's age now is what?

210. Out of 3 females and 3 males, 3 people at random enter an empty room. What is the probability that there are two males and one female in the room now?

ANSWERS

1. A quarter and a nickel

   Be careful of what the wording says: One is not a nickel, but the other is. This is a standard trick in the English language. When you say, "one of them is not a nickel," it doesn't mean that both are not nickels. The key strategy is to pay attention to the wording and not assume anything. The mind gets lured into a process that seems natural. So if you hear someone say, "one of them is not a nickel," you may assume that the person means that both are not nickels. But the statement "one is not a nickel" does not imply that the other cannot be a nickel.

2. **one word**

   Okay, that may be a cheap one! The fact that "one word" in the question was italicized could indicate that the word was in fact "one word."

3. **(a) 30**

   Average rate is not the *average of the rates*, and the answer is not 40. Also, the distance does not need to be known. Where a and b are the two rates, the average rate can be shown to be $2ab/(a + b)$, so $2(20)(60)/(20 + 60) = 30$.

   Detailed explanation: Average rate = Total distance/Total time. Let's say the distance is D one way. Then the total distance is $2D$. Let's say the time the car travels 20 mph is t and the time the car travels 60 mph is T. Then from the formula Rate × Time = Distance, $20 \times t = D$ and $60 \times T = D$. This gives you $t = D/20$ and $T = D/60$. So the total time is $t + T = D/20 + D/60$. This is equal to $t + T = 80D/1,200 = D/15$. So the average rate $= 2D/(t + T) = 2D/(D/15) = 30$.

4. (b) succeeding

   PRE means before; CURS means to run. So, PRECURSORY means to run (or go) before. The opposite is running or going after, or "succeeding."

5. The label BC only could have come into usage after 0 BC.

6. Thirteen nickels, one dime, and one quarter

   The cleverest way to solve this problem is to try to reduce the number of possibilities to a minimum and then figure out all of those possibilities. The highest number of quarters I can have is three, since if I have at least one of every coin, I can't have four quarters (and I can't have more than four quarters because the total would be more than $1). So, if I have three quarters, I am left with fourteen dimes/nickels, which must add up to 25 cents. That's impossible, so suppose I have two quarters. That leaves 50 cents for the dimes/nickels. I can't get fourteen dimes/nickels that add up to 50 cents. So, try one quarter. I have 75 cents left. I can get thirteen nickels and one dime to total 75 cents.

There is also an algebraic way of solving this problem:

Let's say I have n nickels, d dimes, and q quarters. The total number of coins can be represented as:

(Equation 1) $n + d + q = 15$.

The value of all the coins is:

(Equation 2) $5n + 10d + 25q = 100$, since a nickel is worth 5 cents, a dime is worth 10 cents, and a quarter is worth 25 cents.

Let's divide the second equation by 5. We get:

(Equation 3) $n + 2d + 5q = 20$

Multiply Equation 1 by two:

(Equation 4) $2n + 2d + 2q = 30$

Subtract Equation 3 from Equation 4. We get:

(Equation 5) $n - 3q = 10$

Now, because of Equation 2, q must be either 1, 2, 3, or 4 and not more than 4, since n and d must be both positive numbers.

We know from Equation 1 that n must be less than 15, since $d + q$ must be positive numbers.

If $q = 4$, Equation 5 tells us $n = 22$, which is impossible.

If $q = 3$, $n = 19$, which is impossible.

If $q = 2$, $n = 16$, which is impossible.

Therefore, $q = 1$, which makes $n = 13$ and $d = 1$.

Therefore, I have thirteen nickels, one dime, and one quarter.

7. He could type "The file will be deleted."

Think of a statement that will be in conflict with what is mentioned. If the user types "The file will be deleted" and the statement is true, the file's name will change but not be deleted. Thus the statement "The file is deleted" cannot be true. So it is false. But if the statement "The file will be deleted" is false, according to what is mentioned in the question, the file will be deleted, making the user's statement true, which would be contradictory. So if the user types "The file will be deleted," the computer will not be able to perform a function with the file and probably shut down.

8. Terry is 5 years old.

Translate words to math. "Alice was five years older than Terry is now" translates to $a = 5 + T$, where a is the age that Alice was.

Now translate again. Terry is half as old as Alice was: $T = (1/2)a$. Substitute for a:

$T = (1/2)(5 + T)$.

$2T = 5 + T$,

$T = 5$.

So, Terry is 5 years old.

9. Choices (d) negative : positive and (e) disordered : ordered are correct.

An imaginary number is a number such that when multiplied by itself it becomes a negative number. However, there is no way a real number multiplied by itself will give you a negative number. Thus, the term *imaginary*. For example, two times an imaginary number cannot be thought of as greater or less than three times the number. Therefore they are called "not ordered." The real numbers are ordered. For example, three times the number 25 is greater than two times the number 25.

10. 355 × 356 is greater than 354 × 357.

There are more than seven ways to answer this question depending on how your mind works. One strategy is to find a way you can divide to make the problem simpler. The simple way is to divide both quantities by 356 × 354. You then get to compare 357/356 with 355/354. 357/356 = 1 1/356 and 355/354 = 1 1/354. So, the original second quantity is greater than the original first quantity.

11. A single 50 percent discount is better.

It is better to get a single discount of 50 percent. Do not get lured into a process that sounds superficial. In fact, it is always better to get a single discount of the sums of the successive discounts than to get the successive discounts. For example, suppose the item was originally $100. A single discount of 50 percent would give you the item at $50. Now, if I had successive discounts of 20 percent and 30 percent, the first 20 percent discount would give me $80. The second 30 percent discount on $80 would give me $56.

12. If the client died in his sleep, there would be no way of knowing what he was dreaming.

13. Look for something that does not link smoking to cancer directly, but indirectly. That is, something that causes one to smoke and the same thing that causes cancer. So research could find that there is a certain condition that causes one to smoke and the same condition causes one to have cancer. Thus, smoking does not cause cancer; it is the condition that causes it. Unfortunately, that is not the case.

14. (b) 3

Do this problem in steps by starting with two socks. If you get only two socks, they could be different colors, but getting three guarantees that you will have a pair. The strategy is to realize that in order to be sure of what you get, you have to consider the worst-case scenario. The worst case is that if you reach in the drawer, you'll get two different color socks the first two tries—let's say a blue sock and a brown sock the first two tries. But the third try you'll have to get either a blue or a brown sock, which will make a pair with one of the first two socks.

15. **Thursday**

The key is to realize that "now" must be Friday. Look for the phrase in the problem that tells you something you can work with and use that with another part of the problem to gradually and stepwise lead to a solution. In the phrase "Two days from now will be Sunday," you can see that *now* must be Friday, since two days from Friday is Sunday. Now look at the phrase "the day before yesterday." *Yesterday* is Thursday since *now* (today) is Friday. "The day before yesterday" is Wednesday, and the "day that follows the day before yesterday" is *Thursday*.

16. **(d) furniture : carpentry tools**

Put MUSIC and VIOLIN in a sentence relating the two words. Music is played on a violin by someone who knows how to play a violin, just as furniture is created by carpentry tools by a person who knows how to use carpentry tools. A crayon is not done with a drawing (drawing is done with a crayon). Note: a symphony is not played on a piano—it is played by an orchestra.

17. (c) 10

There are two alternating sequences: 0, 1, 2, 3, 4, 5 and 0, 2, 4, 6, 8.

18. (e) John Hancock : signature

Look at what is superficial and what is not. George Washington was superficially identified with the cherry tree as John Hancock was superficially identified with his flamboyant signature. All the other people were not superficially identified in the phrase with their name.

19. (b) C minus B is always less than A

Subtract the same thing from both sides. Since the sum of two sides of a triangle must be greater than the third side, A + B > C, so subtracting B from both sides, A > C – B.

20. (c) 19

Use a Venn diagram or write down all the possibilities.

Total number of people:

(a) Blonds without blue eyes (14 − 5 = 9).
(b) Blue-eyed people who are not blond (8 − 5 = 3).
(c) Blue-eyed blonds (5).
(d) People with neither blue eyes or blond hair (2)
Adding a, b, c, and d, we get 9 + 3 + 5 + 2 = 19.

21. (d)

It is very tempting to just subtract the times 9:09 from 10:10, etc., and get 61 minutes, or if you're careless get 101 minutes. However, think of the times closest to one another, 12:12 and 1:01, and you will find the difference is 49 minutes.

22. (c) 5

Draw lines to see that BD is a radius of the circle. The two diagonals of a square will have the same length.

23. (a) 25 × 25 × 25 ×...(where there are fifty 25s)

Try to find a connection between the numbers. You are comparing 50 × 50 × 50 × 50...(100 times) to 100 × 100 × 100 × 100...(50 times). Write 100 as 50 × 2, so now you are comparing 50 × 50 × 50 × 50...(100 times) to 50 × 2 × 50 × 2 × 50 × 2 × 50 × 2...(50 times).You can now cancel 50 × 50 × 50 × 50...50 times from both sides of the comparison. You would then get 50 × 50 × 50 × 50...(50 times) compared with 2 × 2 × 2 × 2...(50 times). You can see the left side of the comparison is 25 × 25 × 25 × 25...(50 times) times the right side.

24. Say IN means NOT, then associate EXTRIC with another word, EXTRACT. So INEXTRICABLE means not extractable—incapable of being extracted—or INSEPARABLE. Association is a powerful strategy for getting the meaning of words.

25. The doctor is the son's mother.

26. If many people paid attention to the ad, it would be very crowded in the early hours. Of course the reason why the ad was put in was because the store did not think that so many people would read the ad.

27. (b) second

Many people who get this problem wrong think of just the numbers, not the wording, assuming that if you overtake the second runner, you are first. But when you overtook the second runner, you took his or her place. Therefore you are now in second place, not first place.

28. (e) none of the above

If the four daughters are those mentioned, think of who the fifth daughter could be—the fifth daughter is Bonnie herself.

29. (e) thimble : finger

   Create a sentence expressing a specific relationship between the capitalized words. HELMET is worn on the HEAD to protect the head, as THIMBLE is worn on the FINGER to protect the finger.

30. If a number is an exact multiple of 9, the sum of the digits of that number is also a multiple of 9. So $1 + 2 + 3 + x = 9$ and $x = 3$.

31. The knight could tear up the paper he picks and offer the other one to the king. He could then tell the king that since the untorn paper reads "Death," the one torn must have read, "Marriage."

32. From first to last: John, Mary, Sarah, Barry

    The easy way to find the answer is to draw the situation with labels for the people's names.

    (1) Sarah is between Barry and Mary: B S M or M S B.
    (2) John is directly in front of Mary: J M
    (3) Mary is in front of two other people: M S B

    So we get from (2) and (3): J M S B

33. One-half the surface area of a ball is greater. Blow up the circle like a balloon to get the ball. One half the surface area of the ball is greater than the area of the circle because the circle is being expanded by being blown up.

34. Write a three-digit number with h hundreds digit, t tens digit, and u units digit as $100h + 10t + u$. You will find that A = 1, B = 0 and C = 9.

    We have $100A + 10B + A - 10C - A = 10A + B$. This gives us $90A + 9B = 10C$ or $10A + B = (10/9)C$.

The only way A and B can be integers is if C = 9. That makes
10A + B = 10. The only way this is possible with A and B as
integers (from 0 to 9) is if A = 1 and B = 0.

35. (b) m

Letters are arranged in pairs, backward skipping every third
letter: m n (o) p q (r) s t (u) v w (x) y z.

36. 5

Draw a perpendicular line to make a rectangle in the figure
and you will also have a 3-4-5 triangle.

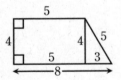

A powerful strategy in geometry is to draw extra lines to get
more information from the problem. You may not remember
this, but when you first took geometry, one of the first proofs
that the teacher probably showed was "if two sides of a triangle are equal, then the base angles are equal." The teacher
drew a perpendicular line to start the proof—unfortunately

the teacher probably did not tell you that the reason she did this was because when you draw something you get more information and are able to start solving the problem. A natural phenomenon! So in this problem, draw a line to make a rectangle in the figure and you will find that you will have a 3-4-5 triangle.

$x = 5$.

37. (c) 40 percent

Translate words to math. *Percent* can be translated to 1/100, *of* to X, *what* to x, *is* to =.

$A = [250/100](B)$.

$x/100 (A) = B$.

Substitute: $x/100[(250/100)]B = B$.

Cancel B: $x/100[250/100] = 1$. $250x/10000 = 1$ so $x = 10{,}000/250 = 40$.

38. The average rate is less than the average of the rates.

Average rate = 2AB/(A + B).

Average of the rates = (A + B)/2.

Detailed solution:

From the formula of Rate × Time = Distance, calling the time for the car to go uphill, t, and the time for the car to go downhill, T, with D being the distance downhill and uphill,

(1) A × t = D and

(2) B × T = D.

Now, Average rate = Total distance/Total time.

So,

(3) Average rate = 2D/(t + T).

From (1) we have

(4) t = D/A

and from (2) we have

(5) T = D/B

Substituting from (4) and (5) in (3), we get

(6) Average rate = 2D/(D/A + D/B)

This becomes

(7) Average rate = 2AB/(A + B)

But the average of the rates is just (A + B)/2. So we ask, is

2AB/(A+B) greater, equal to, or less than (A+B)/2?

So we compare

2AB/(A+B) with (A+B)/2.

Put 2AB/(A+B) under a Column A and (A+B)/2 under a Column B and let's compare the Columns:

Column A	Column B
$\dfrac{2AB}{A+B}$	$\dfrac{A+B}{2}$

Now multiply both columns by 2 and then by (A + B). We get

Column A	Column B
4AB	(A + B) (A + B)

This becomes

Column A	Column B
4AB	A × A + 2AB + B × B

Now subtract 4AB from both columns.
We get:

Column A	Column B
0	A × A – 2AB + B × B

But A × A – 2AB + B × B = (A – B)(A – B) so we get:

Column A	Column B
(A – B)	(A – B)

Since we are told that A and B are *different* rates, A − B cannot be 0, and so (A − B)(A − B) is always greater than 0 whether A is greater than B or less than B. So Column B is greater than Column A and the original quantity in Column B, the average of the rates, is greater than the original quantity in Column A, the average rate.

39. e, a, c, b, d

40. (e) 13

Almost everyone who tries this problem gets it wrong! To get the right answer, you have to visualize something that is not straightforward.

When this problem first appeared in the *Washington Post* and other newspapers throughout the country in 1995, forty percent of people answered (a) 9 because they just added the small triangles in the figure, ABC, BDE, BEC, etc. Twenty-five percent of people answered (b)10 because they added the small triangles in the figure and also added the big triangle AGJ. Eight percent of people answered (c) 11 because they added the small triangles, the big triangle AGJ, and triangle

ADF. Sixteen percent chose (f) none of the above, many of whom merely guessed at an answer without really working it out. Seven percent of people chose the correct answer, (e) 13, because they added the small triangles, the big triangle, triangle ADF, and the triangles BGI and CHJ.

Note: Four percent of people chose (d) 12—they were almost correct. They added the small triangles, the big triangle, and triangle ADF but then only added the triangle BGI and not also CHJ.

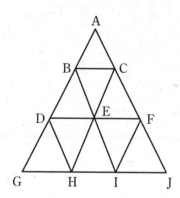

41. When the bird flies, it pushes down on the air, which pushes down on the scale. The scale reads the same.

42. (e) cannot be determined because this is an ambiguous question

How can you overtake the person who is last?

43. (b) 202/962 is greater. Add 208/962 to both quantities and compare.

44. (e) termite : house

Create a sentence expressing a specific relationship between the capitalized words.

MOTH is a living thing that destroys CLOTHING, as termite is a living thing that destroys a house.

45. (a) No good person lives to an old age and (d) All bad people do not die young. "Only the good die young" means that those who are not good do not die young and no good person does not die young. Choice (c) Only bad people do not die young would have been correct if all people were either good or bad. Some may be neither.

46. (e) Phil could give Harry $20 and could give Sam $10.

This could really give you a headache if you don't represent what's given in a table.

	H	S	P	
Harry owes Sam $30	+$30	–$30		Harry is ahead $30 and Sam is behind $30
Sam owes Phil $20		+$20	–$20	Sam is ahead $20 and Phil is behind $20
Phil owes Harry $50	–$50		+$50	Phil is ahead $50 and Harry is behind $50
Total	–$20	–$10	+$30	Phil must give Harry $20 and Sam $10 to make totals 0

47. (d) I and II only

    If nobody loves nobody, then it is like saying nobody loves zero people. So they must love more than zero people. Then somebody loves somebody and everybody loves somebody.

48. (e) 2 × 6 × 36

    When you have to choose something different from the rest of other choices, look for either something all the other choices have that the correct one doesn't, or something that the correct choice has that the other choices don't have. So don't multiply: Notice that all choices are divisible by 5 except choice (e), 2 × 6 × 36. Also, (e) 2 × 6 × 36 is the only choice that is divisible by 9.

49. (c) 37 percent

The equivalent single discount is less than the sum of the discounts. Start with $100. A 30 percent discount gives you a $70 price. A 10 percent discount on $70 gives you a price of $63. $100 − $63 = $37 discount, which is equivalent to a 37 percent discount on $100.

50. 25°

To find the solution, label all the angles with angle BEC = x.

Let $\angle AEB = y$, $\angle BEC = x$, and $\angle CED = z$.

Since $\angle AED = 90$, (1) $x + y + z = 90$.

Since $\angle BED = 40$, (2) $x + z = 40$.

Since $\angle AEC = 75$, (3) $y + x = 75$. Subtracting Equation (2) from Equation (1) we get $y = 50$. Substituting $y = 50$ in Equation (3) we get $x = 25$.

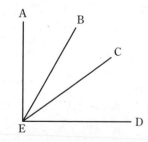

51. 999 × 1,001 is just 1 less than 1,000 × 1,000.

   One of the key strategies in mathematics is to write what is presented in a different form: Write 999 × 1,001 as $(1,000 - 1) \times (1000 + 1)$ and you'll find that's equal to $1,000 \times 1,000 - 1$, since $(a - 1) \times (a + 1) = a \times a - 1$.

52. 276

   Each person can shake hands with 23 other people, so we have 24 × 23 possible combinations. But because it takes two people to make a handshake, we must divide this product by 2, so we get (24 × 23)/2, or 276.

53. DRAW is the only verb on the list with a past tense that does not rhyme with OUGHT.

   The strategy is to try to see something curious in the words. Notice something that many of the words have in common. Most of them have a past tense that has a different structure or sound from the word. BRING—not "BRINGED" but BROUGHT, BUY—not "BUYED" but BOUGHT,

CATCH—not "CATCHED" but CAUGHT, etc. And all of these past tense words rhyme with OUGHT, *except* "DREW," which is the past tense of DRAW. So DREW is the odd man out!

54. (b)

There is one right angle in the first set for each figure and two right angles in each figure in the second set. So the missing figure must have two right angles.

55. There are actually several correct answers to this problem. Here are some of them:

A-E-T makes EAT, TEA, and ATE;

A-T-R makes ART, RAT, and TAR;

O-T-P makes OPT, TOP, and POT;

A-P-T makes APT, PAT, and TAP;

R-E-A makes EAR, ARE, and ERA.

The thing to do is to figure out how to start a problem like this. What do you do first? First, just try to make a three-letter word—any three-letter word, like TIN. Using those letters, T-I-N, can you make another word? Start with T: TNI does not make a word. Now methodically use I as the first letter: INT and ITN do not make a word. Now start with N: NIT and NTI do not make a word—so T-I-N does not work.

Don't get discouraged. Try another three-letter word: E-A-T.

EAT is a word. Start with A now: ATE is a word. Now start with T: TEA is a word. Other correct answers are OPT, TOP, POT, and ART, RAT, and TAR.

56. The only number that meets these requirements is 735.

57. The only English word that can be formed by two consecutive three-letter abbreviations for months is DECOCT, which means to extract the flavor by boiling or to steep in hot water.

58. AD × CD is greater than h × AB.

To solve, *label* the sides of the parallelogram with letters like a and b, then *cancel* the like quantities.

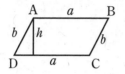

h × AB = h × a and AD × CD = b × a

We are then comparing h × a with b × a. Since the a is the same in each expression, we are really comparing h with b, and h is less than b because b is the largest side (the hypotenuse) of a right triangle. Thus the original h × AB is less than AD × CD.

59. The long hand passes the short hand only eleven times. The long hand passes the short hand at noon, and between the times 1 PM and 2 PM, 2 PM and 3 PM, 3 PM and 4 PM, 4 PM and 5 PM, 5 PM and 6 PM, 6 PM and 7 PM, 7 PM and 8 PM, 8 PM and 9 PM, 9 PM and 10 PM, 10 PM and 11 PM a total of eleven times. Note that the long hand does not pass the short hand between 11 PM and 12 AM, it just meets the short hand at 12 AM.

60. One word is PASSIVE. When the prefix IM is placed before that word, creating the word IMPASSIVE, that word has the same meaning. Other pairs are RAVEL-UNRAVEL, FLAMMABLE-INFLAMMABLE, and VALUABLE-INVALUABLE.

61. I know that you probably were trying to figure out the sides and the relationship of all the lengths AC, AB, BD, and CE. But what you probably didn't think of is that the *area* of triangle ABC is represented as CE × AB/2 *but also* as BD × AC/2. So (1) CE × AB = BD × AC. Now if AC is greater than AB (given), in order for (1) to be true, CE must be greater than BD!

62. 24

    (3 × 4 × 2)

63. (c) 4,100

    $1,000 + 40 + 1,000 + 30 + 1,000 + 20 + 1,000 + 10 = 4,100.$

64. (d) p

Look for a relationship between the letters. Between a and b there are no letters. Between b and d there is one letter (c), Between d and g there are two letters (e, f). Between g and k there are three letters (h, i, j). To continue the pattern, skip four letters (l, m, n, o). The next letter in the sequence is p.

65. 666

The integers between 0 and 1000 that are exactly divisible by 3 are 3, 6, 9, 12, 15, 18... You can see that there are $999/3 = 333$ integers between 0 and 1000 that are exactly divisible by 3. The integers between 0 and 1000 are 1, 2, 3... 999. This is a total of $999 - 1 + 1 = 999$ integers. Thus $999 - 333 = 666$.

66. 100

Don't be careless. Watch what you are dividing. You're not dividing by 2, you are dividing by 1/2. So you have to know your basic skills. Diving by 1/2 is like multiplying by two. So the answer is $(40 \times 2) + 20 = 80 + 20 = 100$.

67. (c) trout : fish

You may have thought the answer was (a), but a TURTLE is a *creature*, which is a type of REPTILE, as trout is a *creature*, which is a type of fish.

68. 1. *please*
    2. *ground*
    3. *around*
    4. *knight*
    5. *fright*
    6. *danger*

Here are some more:

7. *trivet*

8. *strove*

9. *shovel*

10. *slight*

11. *mother*

12. *craven*

69. c, e, a, d, b

70. (c) U

In set I, all three symbols are represented by straight lines. In set II, the two symbols are represented by straight and curved lines.

71. (b) 2

One of them is not 2, it is 1. But the other is 2.

72. The triangle shown has a base of 6 and sides 2 and 4. Since 2 + 4 = 6, the triangle has collapsed into a straight line. On this line, the line segment labeled x must be 1.

73. 28

Lowest average score = $[21 \times 80 + (60 - 21) \times 0]/60 = 28$

74. 640

$(9 \times 6 \times 3)x = 6 \times 12 \times 4 \times 12 \times 2.5 \times 12; x = 640$

75. 7/16 is greater.

Multiply 16×3 and 7×7 in the fractions. $48 < 49$ so $3/7 < 7/16$.

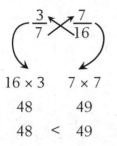

$$16 \times 3 \qquad 7 \times 7$$
$$48 \qquad 49$$
$$48 \quad < \quad 49$$

76. You can simplify the problem by multiplying the numerator and the denominator by the same number. This process will not change the value of the original fraction. So, multiply both numerator and denominator by 4 and you get 4,444 divided by 100, which is 4,444 percent.

77. Roots are a powerful tool in figuring out the meaning of words. The root MAN means "hand." The root MIT means "to send." So MANUMIT means to send by hand or set free.

78. (a) n

There are actually two sequences here: a (b) c (d) e (f) g (h) i...and z (y) (x) w (v) (u) t (s) (r) q (p) (o) n...

79. (e) 7

If people are denoted by a, b, c, you have committees a, b, c, ab, ac, bc, and abc.

80. (a) 11/20

81. 21

Represent $b = a + 2$, $c = a + 4$, so $a + b + c = 3a + 6 = 57$. If $3a = 51$, $a = 17$, so $c = a + 4 = 21$.

82. 400

   Let n be the number of original shelves. Then $80n = 50(n + 3)$. $30n = 150$; $n = 5$. $80 \times 5 = 400$.

83. An hourglass

84. No water—it would be all strained out.

85. 35 × 65 is greater. Divide both products by 65 × 34. You then only have to compare 35/34 with 66/65. Since 35/34 = 1 1/34 and 66/65 = 1 1/65, the first product in the question is greater.

86. (f) 36

   The final result must be divisible by 9. It is very interesting that when you add the digits of a number and subtract that from the original number you get a number that is a perfect multiple of 9. Here's the proof: Represent the two-digit number as $10t + u$ where t is the tens digit and u is the units digit. Adding the digits, we get $t + u$. Subtracting from the original number, we get $10t + u - t - u = 9t$. Since t is an integer, the only choice that fits is (f) 36. What's more interesting is that any number that is a multiple of 9 has digits that add up to a multiple of 9.

Here's a great parlor trick: Have someone choose a number. Then have that person add the digits. Then have the person subtract that result from the original number to get a final result. Have the person now cross out one of the digits in the final answer. You will be able to tell the person what digit he crossed out if he tells you the remaining digit. For example, he starts with 23. $2 + 3 = 5$. $23 - 5 = 18$. He crosses off the 8. He is left with 1. You will be able to tell the digit crossed out. Why?

Any number that is a multiple of 9 has digits that add up to a multiple of 9. So whatever number you crossed out, the crossed-out number must be 9 minus the number left!

87. The mind may give you the pronunciation of DOUS as "doos." Don't assume that is the correct pronunciation. Realizing that, you may come up with the words *stupendous, tremendous, or horrendous.*

88. (e) a country

    MEANYRG spells GERMANY.

89. (d) Spaceship

    Look for similarities in the messages: *Avion* occurs in (1) and (2) and so does *Serious*. So *Avion* must mean *Serious*. *Balcon* appears in (1) and (3) and so does *Fumes*. So *Balcon* must mean *Fumes*. So looking at (1), *Sondor* must mean *Spaceship*.

90.   (d) 240

Do this in steps: If eight people can wash 50 cars in 60 hours, then four people can wash 50 cars in 120 hours. It would take twice as much time to wash, since there are half as many people to wash. Thus, it would take four people 240 hours, twice as long, to wash 100 cars, since there are twice as many cars now.

91.   (c) cannot be determined as true or false

Translate to something you know. For example, let Blips be Students and Plips be Teachers. And let Jips be Actors. So "Some students are actors" is neither false nor true.

92.   (c) 99

This is tricky. If Matt is the fiftieth fastest runner, he would be number 50 in the sequence 1, 2, 3…50. To be the fiftieth slowest, he'd have to be number 50 in the sequence 50, 51, 52…99, since there are fifty numbers from 50 to 99 inclusive.

93. (d) None of the above can be proved true.

Write P > N and D < P. This is the same as P > N and P > D. You cannot determine the relationship of D and N. For example, if P is be 6', N can be 5', and D can be 5.5' or N can be 5' and D can be 5' or N can be 5.5' and D can be 5.5'.

94. (d) 24

Write the number of fish Harry caught as H and the number of fish Sam caught as S. Then translate to math: (1) $H = 3S$. So, (2) $H + S = 32$. Substitute $H = 3S$ in (2) and we get $3S + S = 32$. $4S = 32$, $S = 8$. So, $H = 3S = 24$.

95. (c) 10

Draw a diagram to illustrate the situation.

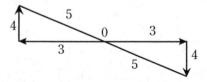

The distance between the two runners is 10.

96. MAINE is the shortest name of a state that shares a letter in common with each of the other fifty states

97. 24

Start with the first person, *a*, at the left side in a corner position. Then figure out the combinations you can have (*ab-cd* or *ac-bd*, etc.) Since *a* is in the left corner, you can play around with combinations of *bcd* for the remaining positions. There are 3 × 2 = 6 of them. Now *b*, *c*, or *d* can be in the left corner also, so there are 6 + 6 + 6 more combinations. That gives us a total of 24.

98. No

Watch the wording. A widow has lost her husband. His widow would be his present wife, but he is dead, so that's impossible. If the wording said "a widow's sister," then it would be possible, since he would not be her dead husband.

99. 9

You may have thought of subtracting 9 from 17, giving you 8. But the question says "all but 9 die." That means you have 9 left!

100. (d) 201

Place 11 cartons with the 40" side along the back of the room, and repeat in front of this row so you have 15 rows deep of 11 cartons wide (165 cartons). In the remaining space, place two cartons with their 48" side against the back and make 18 rows of these (36 cartons). This gives 165 + 36 = 201 refrigerators stored. You can also get 201 fridges in by changing the numbers so you have 15 rows of 5 cartons and 18 rows of 7 cartons.

101. Quantity B

Understand the difference between "average rate" and the "average of the rates." Then *cross-multiply*, then *subtract 4ab* from both quantities.

Detailed explanation: The average rate of a car going uphill at a miles per hour and downhill at b miles per hour the same distance is just $2ab/(a + b)$. Proof: Call the distance d. Call the time it takes for the car to go uphill t. Call the time it takes for the car to go downhill the same distance, d, T. Because Rate × Time = Distance,

(1) $a \times t = d$

(2) $b \times T = d$

The average rate is the total distance divided by the total time. That is $2d/(t + T)$.

Using (1), we get $t = d/a$ and (2), $T = d/b$.

So $2d/(t + T) = 2d/(d/a + d/b)$, which can be seen to be just $2ab/(a + b)$.

The average of the rates a and b is just $(a + b)/2$.

So Quantity A is just $2ab/(a + b)$ and

Quantity B is just $(a + b)/2$.

Multiply both quantities by 2. You get

Quantity A: $4ab/(a + b)$

Quantity B: $a + b$

Now multiply both quantities by $(a + b)$.

You get

Quantity A: $4ab$

Quantity B: $(a + b) \times (a + b) = a^2 + b^2 + 2 \times b \times a$

Now subtract $4ab$ from both quantities. You get

Quantity A: 0

Quantity B: $a^2 - 2 \times b \times a + b^2 = (a - b) \times (a - b)$

Since a is not equal to b, $(a - b) \times (a - b)$ is always greater than 0.

Thus Quantity A is less than Quantity B and so the original Quantity A $[2ab/(a + b)]$ is less than the original Quantity B $[(a + b)/2]$. Thus, the average rate of the car going uphill at a miles per hour and downhill at b miles per hour is less than the average of the rates a and b.

102. (b) Mike is a child.

103. Small

Adding *er* gives you *smaller*. You can also do this with *meter*. Adding *milli* makes the word *millimeter*, which is smaller.

104. Yes

Don't get lured by the fact that the fourth of July is a holiday celebrated only in the United States. It doesn't say *celebrated* or *holiday* in the question. So of course they have a fourth of July (July 4) in England, since that's also a day in their calendar.

105. One

Analyze what a birthday is. Don't get lured into the word *average*. It's a single day that someone was born. So the average man (or any man) has only *one* birthday, his date of birth.

106. 6

You may have thought the answer was "three outs." But there are *two* teams that play in an inning. So there are *six outs*.

107. See what you have been given to work with in answering the question. Since the problem doesn't give any indication of the butcher's weight, the word *weigh* must refer to something else. The butcher weighs *meat*!

108. (e)

The ? must have only one set of parallel lines.

109. 12 stamps

You may have multiplied 2 × 12 to get 24. But a dozen stamps means 12 stamps no matter how much each stamp is worth!

110. 60 minutes

Many of you probably think that I should multiply 3 pills by 30 minutes to give me 90 minutes. But think of how you take the pills. I take the first pill, and in a half-hour I take the second pill, and then in the next half-hour I take the third pill. So the number of minutes that pass from the first to the third pill is 60 minutes.

111. Ten numbers

Start with the lowest number: 4,567. The next number is 4,568, then 4,569; 4,578; 4,579; 4,589; 4,678; 4,679; 4,689; 4,789. So there are ten numbers.

112. 1

Note that the numbers in the sequence are integers multiplied by themselves three times, that is $125 = 5 \times 5 \times 5$; $64 = 4 \times 4 \times 4$; $27 = 3 \times 3 \times 3$; $8 = 2 \times 2 \times 2$. So the next number would be 1.

113. (e) 45

If John = 10, then his mother is 40. When John is 15, he is 5 years older. So, his mother must be 5 years older, and then is 45.

114. (a) 6

You need to use the formula Rate × Time = Distance, that is $r \times t = d$. For the uphill trip,

r (uphill) × t (uphill) = 1 mile

For the downhill trip,

r (downhill) × t (downhill) = 1 mile

The average rate of the car is the total distance traveled (2 miles) divided by the total time traveled, t (uphill) + t (downhill).

Since the average rate was given as 20 mph, 20 = 2 divided by [t (uphill) + t (downhill)]. Thus, we get 10 = t (uphill) + t (downhill).

115. (d) You can't do anything.

Since you're going from a very high speed to 0 (when the elevator hits the ground) the force is tremendous (from physics, force is proportional to the acceleration). You can't jump up because you'd be going from a very high speed to a speed of less than 0 and that would also require a tremendous force. The force is what gets you, so there's nothing you can do!

116. 46 × 767 × 72 is less than 767 × 46 × 74.

Cancel 46 and 767 (common numbers) from both products.

117. The house **that** is painted yellow has just been sold.
The house, **which** is painted yellow, has just been sold.

In (1), "The house" refers to one of a number of houses. In (2), "The house" does not refer to one of a number of houses.

118. Seven

Draw a line in the circle and place nine people on the line. Choose two people on the line and draw another circle inside the first so that those two people are on the circumference of that circle. Thus you would have to move the rest of the people (7 people) to place them also on the circumference of that circle.

119. 1 is greater.

Multiply 1 by 99/77 and compare that with 77/99.

120. (b) replace...important

Use key words: *while, is not able, it is still able.*

121. It confuses people with playing styles.

122. (e) freezing : spoilage

A VACCINATION is used to prevent a DISEASE as freezing is used to prevent spoilage. Note that aspirin is not used to prevent a headache; it can be used to reduce the symptoms of a headache and also as a regiment to prevent against heart attacks.

123. 7:04 AM

The clock gains 3 minutes every day, or 1 minute every 8 hours. Between 11 PM Sunday night and Tuesday morning 7 AM is 24 + 8 hours. So the clock gains 4 minutes.

124. Average speed is total distance divided by total time. So for the first half, 25 = 50/time of first half. Thus the time for first half is 2 hours. For Phil to average 50 miles per hour for the whole trip, we would get 50 = 100/time for the whole trip. Time for the whole trip then is 2 hours. That would mean that Phil must go an infinite speed the second half of the trip to go 50 miles in 0 hours.

125. (c) 3 vs. 3

Label the 9 coins *a, b, c, d, e, f, g, h, i*. First weigh *abc* with *ghi*. If they balance, then heavy coin is *d, e,* or *f*. So weigh *d* with *e*. If they balance, then the heavy coin is *f*. If they don't balance, then whichever coin tips the scale is the heavy one. Suppose *abc* and *ghi* do not balance. Then whichever side tips the scale has the heavier coin. Suppose in this case the side with *ghi* has the heavy coin. Then, in the procedure done before, weigh *g* with *h*. If they balance, then *i* is heavy. If they don't balance, then the coin that tips the scale downward is heavy.

Here is a more sophisticated solution:

Number the coins 1 through 9. In the first weighing, place coins 1, 2, and 3 on the left side of the scale, and place 4, 5, and 6 on the right side. Leave 7, 8 and 9 on the side. For the second weighing, regardless of the results of the first, place coins 1, 4, and 7 on the left, and place 2, 5, and 8 on the right. The following chart demonstrates how to determine which is the heaviest coin depending on these results. In this chart, the results displayed list which side of the balance scale was heavier.

Heavy Coin	Results of <u>First</u> <u>Weighing</u> 1, 2, 3, vs. 4, 5, 6	Results of <u>Second</u> <u>Weighing</u> 1, 4, 7, vs. 2, 5, 8
1	Left	Left
2	Left	Right
3	Left	Equal
4	Right	Left
5	Right	Right
6	Right	Equal
7	Equal	Left
8	Equal	Right
9	Equal	Equal

126. He or she should open the remaining door.

The probability would be 2/3, not 1/2! Many people have thought that there is a 1/2 chance of having the car behind the door the contestant chose since there are two doors. However, because you have chosen a door first, out of three, there is a 1/3 probability there is a car behind it, and there would be a 2/3 probability any other door has the car behind it. So if you chose two of the other doors, you would have a 2/3 probability of the car. And if one door was eliminated by the host, since that door had the goat, if you switched doors, then it would be in effect as if you were choosing two doors, which would give you the 2/3 probability that the car was behind the remaining door.

Another explanation:

Interestingly enough, the answer is that the contestant should switch doors, because there is actually a 2/3 chance of winning the car by switching, while there is only a 1/3 chance of winning the car if the contestant opens his or her original door!

This is how most people's minds approach the problem: The host eliminates one door with the goat, so there is a goat or a car behind the contestant's door. So the probability is 1/2. And it doesn't matter whether the contestant opens his or her original door or changes doors. But let's see what is really happening. The probability of having a car behind the contestant's door when he or she originally chooses the door is 1/3, since there are three doors and only one door that has a car behind it. And there is a 2/3 probability that the car is behind one of the other two doors (since there are two ways a car can be behind one of the remaining doors [car-goat; goat-car] out of a total of three possibilities: car-goat; goat-car; goat-goat). Now, if the host eliminates a door, there would still be the 1/3 probability that the car was behind the contestant's original door—so once a door is eliminated, there is a 2/3 probability the car was behind the remaining door.

I have pondered the *Let's Make a Deal* problem for some time, and I came to the conclusion that it is 2/3 when I took a more dramatic variation of the problem. Suppose I had 100 doors and 1 of them had a car behind it. The rest had goats. If I chose one door, there would no doubt be a 1/100 chance that there was a car behind it. So the remaining doors combined would have a 99/100 chance of the car. Now no matter what was done to the other doors, there would still be a 1/100 chance of the car's being behind the door that was chosen. So if the host knew that 98 of the doors did not have the car, and then eliminated those doors, the remaining door then must have had a 99/100 chance that there was a car behind it.

Suppose you had 100 doors. The chance of the car's being behind the contestant's chosen door is 1/100, obviously a very slim chance that won't change even when the host eliminates 98 doors. When the doors are eliminated, and all but two are left, the contestant still has chosen a door with a very, very slim chance the car is behind it, namely 1/100. Because the host knows where the car is (and where the goats are), and because 98 of the goats were eliminated, the remaining door has a (98 + 1)/100 chance there is a car behind it.

Note that initial reasoning may indicate that when there is only one door left, since 98 doors have been eliminated, the total number of possibilities for what's behind the contestant's

door is two, a car or a goat. The favorable number of possibilities is one, the car. So by strict definition of probability,
the probability is 1/2 no matter what the host knows or did.
But according to the previous paragraph, that is not the case.

I think probability has a somewhat ambiguous definition, es-
pecially if there is "conditional" probability, but it seems that
if you tried the 100 doors out you would in fact find you'd get
a 1/100 chance of getting the car.

127. $X = w$; $Y = h$; and $Z = t$: where there were.

128. 43

Call x the number of boxes with 6 donuts, y the number
of boxes with 9 donuts, and z the number of boxes with 20
donuts. Then the total number of donuts, N, for x, y, z boxes
is represented by $N = 6x + 9y + 20z$, or $N = 3(2x + 3y) + 20z$.
Now $x = 0, 1, 2, 3$ etc., $y = 0, 1, 2, 3$, etc., $z = 0, 1, 2, 3$, etc.

$20z$ can be 20, 40, 60, etc.

$3(2x + 3y)$ can be 0, 6, 9, 12, 15, 18, 21, 24, 27, and any
multiple of 3 thereafter.

So all the combinations become: 0, 6, 9, 12, 15, 18, 21, 24, 26, 27, 29, 30, 32, 33, 35, 36, 38, 39, 40, 41, 42, 44 (which is 20 + 24), 45, 46 (which is 40 + 6), 47 (which is 20 + 27), 48, 49 (which is 40 + 9), 50 (which is 20 + 30), 51, etc., and all consecutive numbers thereafter. The greatest number that you cannot make is 43.

129. 2/7

Cross out all the common numerators and denominators. That is, cross out, the 3s, 4s, 5s and 6s. We are left with 2/7. Note that this is a problem that could be done faster *without* a calculator!

130. (d) pygmy : undersized

Suppose you don't know the meaning of the word MENDACIOUS. Mendacious is an adjective probably describing a LIAR. So assume that a LIAR has the characteristic of being mendacious. A pygmy has the characteristic of being undersized. Note that an artist may not be creative.

131. (b) m

Write the sequence as follows: a l b (c, d) e m f (g, h) i n j (k, l). So the next letter is m.

132. 1/3

The favorable outcomes (of spelling an English word) are two: NOT and TON.

The total number of ways of arranging the three letters in a row is six: NTO, NOT, TON, TNO, OTN, ONT. Thus the probability is 2/6 = 1/3.

133. 4,950

This is extremely tricky. Write the numbers as:

1 + 2 + 3 + 4 +...+ 99 = N and then write the numbers below that in reverse:

99 + 98 + 97 + 96 +...+ 1 = N

Adding both sums we get 100 + 100 + 100...(99 times)

This is just 99×100, which is just $2N$.

So $N = 50 \times 99 = 99 \times 100/2 = 4{,}950$

134. 4,951

Look at the first numbers in the parts of the sequence:

First = 1

Second = 2

Third = 4

Fourth = 7

Fifth = 11

Note the first number of the parts of the sequence increase by 1, 2, 3, 4, etc.

(If you add 1 to the first number, you get the second. If you add 2 to the second number, you get the third. If you add 3 to the third number, you get the fourth. If you add 4 to the fourth number, you get the fifth.)

So, the first number, call it N in the nth part of the sequence is

1: $N = 1 + [1 + 2 + 3 + \ldots + (n-1)]$

Now write this again backwards:

2: $N = 1 + [(n-1) + (n-2) + (n-3) + \ldots + 1] + 1$

Adding (1) and (2), we get $2N = 1 + [(1 + n - 1) + (2 + n - 2) + (3 + n - 3) + \ldots + (n - 1 + 1)]$.

This is just equal to $2N = 1 + 1 + [n$ taken $(n - 1)$ times], or just $2 + n(n - 1)$.

So $N = [2 + n(n - 1)]/2$. So, if $n = 100$, then

$N = [2 + 100(99)]/2 = [2 + 9,900]/2 = 4,951$

135. 70°

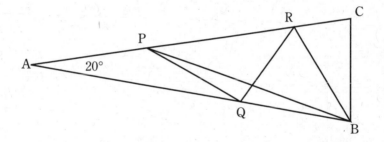

Make isosceles triangles: Where R is on AC, draw BR = BC; where Q is on AB, draw RQ = RB. Where M is on AC, draw MQ = RQ. We have $\angle BAC = 20°$, $\angle ABC = 80°$, $\angle ACB = 80°$.

You can find that:

$\angle BRC = 80°$, $\angle RBC = 20°$, $\angle QBR = 60°$, $\angle RQB = 60°$, $\angle QRB = 60°$, $\angle QRM = 40°$, $\angle QMR = 40°$, and $\angle MQR = 100°$.

Note: $\angle MQA = 20°$ and $\angle A = 20°$, so AM = MQ. But MQ = AP, since BC = AP and BC = MQ. Thus, AM = MQ, and so point M coincides with point P, making M = P. Now since triangle QRB is equilateral, QB = PQ, so $\angle QBP = \angle QPB = 10°$. Since $\angle B = 80°$, $\angle PBC = 70°$.

136. 135°

Rotate the points A, P, and D 90° counterclockwise about B to give the points E, Q, and F respectively. Clearly, $\angle PBQ = 90°$ and QA = PC = 3. By the Pythagorean theorem in triangle PBQ, $PQ^2 = PB^2 + BQ^2 = 2^2 + 2^2 = 8 = QA^2 - AP^2$.

Hence, by the converse of the Pythagorean theorem in triangle PQA, we know that $\angle APQ = 90°$. However, as triangle PBQ is right-angled and isosceles, $\angle BPQ = 45°$.

Therefore, $\angle APB = \angle APQ + \angle BPQ = 90° + 45° = 135°$.

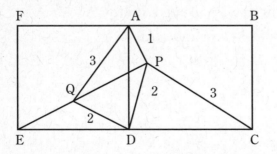

137. (c) flammable and (d) infamous

If we put the prefix *in* in front of each word, the meaning of the word means the opposite of the word, except for *flammable*. (*Inflammable* has the same meaning as *flammable*) and *famous* (*infamous* has the same meaning as *famous*, although *infamous* is *famous* in a bad way).

138. 30°

Draw BG at 20° to BC, cutting CA into CG and GA.

Then, ∠ GBD = 60° and ∠ BGC and ∠ BCG are 80°. So BC = BG.

Also, ∠ BCD = ∠ BDC = 50° so BD = BC = BG, and triangle BDG is equilateral.

But ∠ GBE = 40° = ∠ BEG, so BG = GE = GD.

And ∠ DGE = 40°. Since DG = EG, ∠GDE = ∠ DEG = 70° and since ∠ BEG = 40°, ∠ BED = 30°.

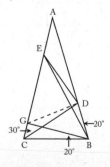

139. (c) 2/3

Probability can be defined as the favorable number of possible outcomes divided by the total number of possible outcomes. Since one of the coins lands as a head, the total number of ways this is possible is the following:

five-cent head, ten-cent tail

five-cent head, ten-cent head

five-cent tail, ten-cent head

There couldn't be a possibility of a ten-cent tail, ten-cent tail combination because we are told that one of the coins must be a head.

So there are three possibilities.

Now, the favorable ways that the five-cent coin will land as a head are:

five-cent head, ten-cent tail

five-cent head, ten-cent head

That is two ways out of three possible ways. Thus, the probability is 2/3.

140. (b) The equivalent discount of each of the three items is between 70 percent and 80 percent.

Suppose we start with a price of $100 for each item. After the first discount, the first item will be $40. After the second discount, the item will be $24. This would represent an equivalent discount of 76 percent. Use the same process for the second and third item. For the second item, we would find that the price after the second discount is $25, which would represent an equivalent discount of 75 percent. For the third item, we would find the equivalent discount to be 79 percent. Thus, (b) is correct.

141. Fill the three-gallon bottle with milk, then pour the three gallons of milk into the five-gallon bottle. Now again fill the three-gallon bottle with milk and pour milk from the three-gallon bottle into the five-gallon bottle until you fill it. You have one gallon left in the three-gallon bottle.

142. FIVE TWO FIVE; TWO FIVE TWO

Spade Spade Club; Spade Spade Club

143. (c) The number of false statements here is three.

If there are three false statements, then C is true and A, B, D, are false.

144. 1,349

Represent the digits as a, b, c, d. So (1) $a = (1/3)b$, (2) $c = a + b$, and (3) $d = 3b$.

From (1) we get (4) $3a = b$. From (3) and (4) we get (5) $d = 9a$. The only way (5) can be true is if $a = 1$, since d is a single digit and not equal to 0, making $d = 9$. Thus, from (1) $b = 3$, and from (2) $c = 4$. So the number $abcd$ is 1,349.

145. They are both lying.

Scenario 1: If the child with brown hair is lying, he is a boy. Then the child with blond hair must be a girl since there is a boy and a girl and thus is also lying.

Scenario 2: If the child with brown hair is not lying, then she's a girl. Since at least one of them is lying, the child with blond hair must be lying and would be a girl also, which is impossible. So the only possibility is the first scenario where both are lying.

146. Method 1: First weigh six balls with six balls. Whichever of the six balls tips the scale, that is where the heavier ball is. So now from those balls, weigh three against three. Again whichever of the three tips the scale is where the heavier ball is. So of the three balls (where one of them is heavier than the other two) weigh one against one. If they balance, the heavier ball is the remaining one. If they don't balance, whichever ball tips the scale is the heavier one.

Method 2: First weigh four balls with four balls. Suppose they balance. Then weigh the remaining four balls—two balls against two balls. Whichever two balls tip the scale downward include the heavier ball. So weigh one of those balls against the other. Whichever ball tips the scale downward is the heavier ball.

Suppose when we weigh the four balls against four balls, they don't balance. The four balls that tip the scale downward have one of the balls that is heavier. So take these four balls and weigh two against two. One of the two balls will tip the scale downward. Whichever of the two balls tips the scale downward contains the heavy ball. Now weigh one of those balls with the other. The one that tips the scale downward is the heavy ball.

Method 3: First weigh three against three. If they balance, then weigh the other three against three. Certainly one side will be heavier so weigh the three balls where one is heavier, one against one. If they balance, it's the remaining ball that is heavier. If they don't balance, the ball that tips the scale downward is heavier.

If the original three against three don't balance, take the three balls that tip the scale downward and weigh two of those balls, one on one side, the other on the other. If they balance, it's the remaining ball. If they don't balance, it's the ball that tips the scale downward.

147. The man is 52 and his wife is 39.

Denote the man's age now as M, the wife's age now as W, the man's age when he was as old as the wife now as m, the wife's age when the man was as old as she is now as w.

Then we get

(1) $M + W = 91$

(2) $m = W$ (since the man was then as old as the wife now)

(3) $M = 2w$ (since the man is twice as old as the wife was)

The key thing to realize is that the difference in ages between the man and his wife now is the same difference then or at any other time. That is,

(4) $M - W = m - w$

So substituting (2) and (3) into (4), we get

$M - W = W - M/2$ or $M - W = (2W - M)/2$, which gives us $2M - 2W = 2W - M$, so we get

(5) $3M = 4W$ or $M = 4W/3$

We substitute (5) into (1) and we get:

$4W/3 + W = 91$; $7W/3 = 91$ and $W = 273/7 = 39$. From (1) we get $M + 39 = 91$, and so $M = 52$.

148. 45/50 or 90 percent

n = nickels, p = pennies, q = quarters, d = dimes

We have $5n + p + 10d + 25q = 100$ (since the total is 100 cents) and $n + p + d + q = 50$ (since the total is 50 coins).

Subtract the two equations:

We get $4n + 9d + 24q = 50$.

Suppose $q = 1$. Then $4n + 9d + 24 = 50$, and so $4n + 9d = 26$.

The only way this is possible is if $d = 2$ and $n = 2$.

Suppose $q = 2$. Then $4n + 9d + 48 = 50$, and we get $4n + 9d = 2$, which is impossible.

So we have 1 quarter, 2 dimes, and 2 nickels, which leaves 45 pennies since the total number of coins is 50. If I drop 1 penny, we have the probability as 45/50 or 90 percent.

149. (e) 108

Translate: The number of apples that Bill bought = B, that Harry bought = H, and that Martin bought = M. "Bill bought four times as many apples as Harry" translates to $B = 4H$. Similarly $B = 3M$. "Bill, Harry, and Martin purchased a total of less than 190 apples" translates to $B + H + M < 190$. You will find that manipulating these equations, we get $B < 120$. However, because H and M are integers, $B = 108$ and not 119!

Here's the complete solution:

(1) $B + H + M < 190$

(2) $B = 4H$

(3) $B = 3M$

Substituting (3) into (1) we get

(4) $3M + H + M < 190$

From (2) and (3), we get

(5) $3M = 4H$ and so

(6) $H = 3M/4$

Substituting (6) into (4) we get

(7) $3M + 3M/4 + M < 190$

This becomes

(8) $19M/4 < 190$ and thus

(9) $M/4 < 10$, so $M < 40$. So at this point you might think that $M = 39$. And from (3), B becomes 117. But from (6) we wouldn't have H as a whole number! The greatest number less than 40 which the whole number M could be for (6) to be true is $M = 36$. Then $H = 27$, and from (3), $B = 108$.

150.

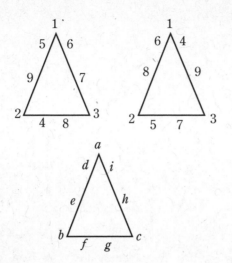

Let's see what numbers would be on the vertices of the triangle. Represent those numbers by *a*, *b*, and *c*. Let the numbers 1 through 9 be represented by *a*, *b*, *c*, *d*, *e*, *f*, *g*, *h*, *i*. Then we have

(1) $a + e + d + b = 17$

(2) $b + f + g + c = 17$

(3) $c + h + i + a = 17$

(4) $a + b + c + d + e + f + g + h + i = 45$ (since all the numbers $1 + 2 + 3...9$ add up to 45)

Adding (1), (2), (3) we get

(5) $2a + 2b + 2c + d + e + f + g + h + i = 51$.

Subtracting (4) from (5) we get $a + b + c = 6$. The only way this can be possible is if the numbers for a, b, and c are 1, 2, 3.

So start with the numbers 1, 2, and 3 at the vertex of the triangle. For the left side, since the numbers must add up to 17, the other two numbers on the left side must add up to 14. The only possibilities are 6 and 8 or 5 and 9. If it is 5 and 9, then the remaining numbers are 4, 6, 7, 8. For the bottom side, two of these numbers (of 4, 6, 7, 8) must add up to $17 - 5 = 12$. The only way is 4 and 8. So then we'd have 6 and 7 left. For the right side, $1 + 3 + 6 + 7$ adds up to 16. Similarly you can see that for the left side 6 and 8 also works and we get the triangle on the right.

151. There are at least four different solutions.

Think outside of the box. Draw lines outside of the square that contains the circles.

Solution 1

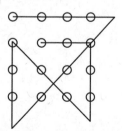

Solution 2

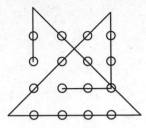

Note that the two ends can be extended to form a continuous path. There are four points external to the 4 × 4 array.

Solution 3

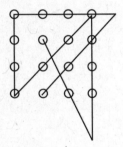

Solution 4

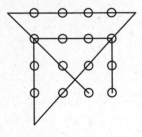

152. (c) There is the same amount of water in the alcohol as alcohol in the water.

Let's say the cup of alcohol you pour in the water contains c gallons (c could be 1/10, for example). Now the water bucket has a mixture of alcohol and water. Now you pour one cup (again, c gallons) of that mixture back into the alcohol bucket. Let's say there are a gallons of alcohol and w gallons of water in that cup. So (1) $a + w = c$.

Now the amount of water poured into the alcohol is w. The amount of alcohol in the water bucket is $c - a$, since we poured a gallons of alcohol into the alcohol bucket from the water bucket. From (1) we get $c - a = w$, so (c) is true.

153. (e) octagon

Here's the figure:

154. (d) e

The sequence is arranged in pairs: st no jk gh

Note that we have a pattern: gh (i) jk (lm) no (pqr) st

The letters in parentheses increase by one letter in the sequence. Thus, the next two letters in the original sequence must be e, f, since the pattern will be preserved:

ef (no letters) gh (i) jk (lm) no (pqr) st

155. $x/2 + y$

You *may have gotten the answer* $x/2 - y$, but that's how many people are left on the bus!

$x - (x/2 - y)$, which is $x/2 + y$, is the answer.

156. LIGHTS, CAMERA, ACTION

157. (b) 2

Write an equation, where n is the number of nickels, d is the number of dimes, and q is the number of quarters: $5n + 10d + 25q = 100$. Start with the smallest numbers for n, d, and q that satisfy the equation. Start with $n = 0$, $d = 0$, then $q = 4$, which is not true since the most q can be is 3. Then try $n = 0$, $d = 1$. Then we get $25q = 90$, which doesn't give us a whole number for q. You will find that if $n = 1$, $d = 2$, and $q = 3$, and if $n = 3$, $d = 1$, and $q = 3$, you will satisfy the equation. So there are two ways to make change.

158. There was no extra dollar.

Watch that your mind doesn't deceive you. They thought the bill came to $30, but that doesn't make it the amount that we want to work with.

159. 95,999

You may have thought the number was 96,666. But then you didn't account for the 9 in the original number. So the least whole number is 95,999.

160. facetious

161. Four states

Hawaii (Honolulu), Oklahoma (Oklahoma City), Indiana (Indianapolis), Delaware (Dover).

162. (d) song : hymn

Put the analogy in a very specific sentence: CHURCH is a religious type of BUILDING as hymn is a religious type of song.

163. **(e) cottage : house**

Put the analogy in a very specific sentence: HAMLET is a small VILLAGE as cottage is a small house.

164. **(e) strength...bored**

The key words are *in spite of*. Look for a contrast or opposites.

165. **(c) shun**

The key word is *moreover*. Not only was Wagner intolerant, but with his "strange behavior," people would avoid (or shun) the composer.

166. (b) feed on poisonous plants

Try to get clues from the rest of the passage and use infer-
ences. Since the fish and shellfish become toxic, it can be
inferred that they must eat the plankton, which could only
be small animals or plants. (a) swim in poisonous water is
incorrect because "coastal plankton" is distinguished in the
sentence from "fishes and shellfish." (d) give off a strange
glow is incorrect because nowhere in the passage does it
mention that the fish give off a "strange glow." Choices (c)
change their feeding habits and (e) take strychnine into
their system are incorrect because it is unlikely that fish and
shellfish would eat sand deposits or glacier or rock forma-
tions—they would eat plants or smaller animals.

167. (e) phenomena of the sea

Pay attention to the three parts of a passage: The opening
sentence leads into what is going to be discussed, the middle
tells us about the passage, and the last sentence or paragraph
usually summarizes or wraps up the passage. Look at the
opening phrase, which introduces the passage. The fact that
glowing water is mentioned indicates that the paragraph preceding the sentence probably talks about the sea.

168. (a) 36

Draw the figure with angle C as a right angle. Now the key strategy is to draw an extra line, BD.

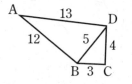

Triangle BCD is then a right triangle and is a 3-4-5 right triangle. Now you have triangle BAD as a 5-12-13 triangle. This is also a right triangle. (In high school you prove these things by using the Pythagorean theorem, but usually students are told to remember certain right triangles like the popular 3-4-5 and 5-12-13 ones.) So if triangle BAD is a right triangle (where angle ABD is a right angle), you can show the area is $(5 \times 12)/2 = 30$. The area of triangle BCD is $(3 \times 4)/2 = 6$, so the total area of the figure is 36.

169. 41

Square $(x + y) = 7$. You get $x^2 + y^2 + 2xy = 49$. Now substitute $xy = 4$.

You get $x^2 + y^2 + 2(4) = 49$. So $x^2 + y^2 + 8 = 49$ and so $x^2 + y^2 = 41$.

170. equal to

Draw the figure and notice that there are two right angles because the sum of the angles of the four-sided figure is 360°.

Since there are then two right triangles, with the use of the Pythagorean theorem, we get

$a^2 + b^2 = c^2 + d^2$. Thus, we find that $a^2 - c^2 = d^2 - b^2$.

171. less than

Compare $2ab$ divided by $(a + b)$ with $(a + b)$ divided by 2 by manipulating the inequality or equality: Multiply both sides by 2 and then by $(a + b)$. Then multiply out $(a + b) \times (a + b)$ and subtract the $4ab$ on the left side from both sides. You will get 0 as compared with $(a - b) \times (a - b)$. Since a is not equal to b (given), 0 is always less than

$(a - b) \times (a - b)$.

172. (a) acclaim...reservations

The key words are *even though*. This signals a contrast.

173. (e) car : garage

A SHIP is put in a HARBOR as a car is put in a garage. Although bird is put in a nest, the analogy presents the ideas in the reverse order, and a nest is not put in a bird.

174. 50

Draw lines to get additional information.

175. (b) tranquil

One strategy is when the word sounds "big" like *effervescent*, *magnanimous*, and *scintillating*, it probably will mean something big or flashy. Think of *ebullient* as a big-sounding word. The opposite would be *tranquil*.

176. 30

From 10 to 100, you have 12, then 15, etc., up to 99. This is 4 × 3, 5 × 3, up to 33 × 3. So there are 33 − 4 + 1 = 30 integers.

177. 36

The edge of the cube is 3 and there are 12 edges.

178. (e) o

a c d b e g h i f j l m n o k

⟵⟶ ⟵⟶ ⟵⟶

179. 3

In 4 hours Jim can do one job, and in 4 hours Tom can do two jobs.

180. (a) 30

Total number of people = Number who can write with both hands + Number who can write with only the left hand + Number who can write with only the right hand. Or, 50 = 10 + 20 + x. Thus x = 20 can write with only the right hand. But 10 can write with both the left and right hand, so 30 can write with the right hand.

181. cannot be determined

Translate words to math. We have $(10 + x)/2$ divided by $(10 + x) = 1/2$. So we get

$$\frac{10 + x}{[2\,(10 + x)]} = 1/2$$

Cancel $(10 + x)$: we get $1/2 = 1/2$.

Thus, x cannot be determined.

182. (b) 84

$96 - 12 = 84$

183. 4,400 feet

In one revolution the wheel would roll one circumference or $2\pi r$ feet $= 2\pi$ feet.

$2\pi \times 700 = 1,400\pi = 4,400$ feet (approximately).

184. 33 1/3 percent

$$(80 - 60) \times \frac{100}{60} = 33 \text{ } 1/3 \text{ percent}$$

185. 150 square inches

$$186 - 2 \times (6 \times 3) = 150$$

186. c, e, a, b, d *or* e, a, b, d, c

187. (e) tournament : joust

LITIGATION is done in a COURT as joust is done in a tournament.

188. (b) 28

Using symbols, let $S = 3W$. $S + W =$ Number of string and wind musicians. Thus, $3W + W = 4W$ is the number of string and wind musicians. The only choice where W is a whole number is where $4W = 28$ ($W = 7$).

189. (a) viola : cello

OBOE and BASSOON are in the same family of instruments—woodwinds—as viola and cello are in the same family of instruments—strings.

190. 120

Write a relation: $C = 4S$, $C = 3W$, $C + S + W < 200$.

191. Jane, Ellen, Ann, Joyce

Translate from words to math:

$Ja = 3A,$

$A - 3 = Jo - 1,$

$E = 2A.$

So, $Ja = 3A$, $A = Jo + 2$, $E = 2A$, so $Ja > E > A > Jo$

192. Six

$3Sw + 2Sk = 3Sk$. So, $3Sw = 1Sk$.

193. (e) I, II, and III

Where x is a whole number, the number of beads is $3x + 2$ since you are left with only a red and a white and all the rest are red, white, and green. Thus, see if x is a whole number where $3x + 2 = 17$, 29, and 35. Alternate solution: If the order is red, white, green..., then the number of beads you have ending in white is $r, w = 2; r, w, g, r, w = 5; r, w, g, r, w, g, r, w = 8$, so the sequence is 2, 5, 8, 11, 14, 17, 20, 23, 26, 29, 32, 35.

194. d, b, e, a, c

195. (b) barcarole : gondola

LULLABY is sung to a person in a CRADLE, and barcarole is sung to a person in a gondola.

196. (f) I and V only

The statement implies the following possibilities: Susan, but not Freddie will be hired; Freddie, but not Susan will be hired; and neither Freddie nor Susan will be hired. Statement (I) and (V) are equivalent and possible. (II) is true. (III) is false. (IV) is false.

197. (b) less than 30

Draw a line that makes the third side of the triangle with sides 4 and 5.

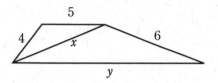

The sum of the lengths of two sides of a triangle must be greater than the third side. So, $4 + 5 > x$ and $x + 6 > y$. Thus, since $9 > x$, we can set up a single inequality and add 6 to both sides to get $15 > x + 6$. But $x + 6 > y$, so $15 > x + 6 > y$, and so $15 > y$. The perimeter of the figure is $4 + 5 + 6 + y = 15 + y$. Since $15 > y$, $15 + y$ (the perimeter) is less than 30.

198. The fractions are equal. They are both equal to 2/1.

199. (b) "I will be shot."

If he says, "I will be shot," that statement is neither true nor false. If it were true, he would be hanged. But then "being shot" wouldn't have been true. Thus, the statement must be false. But if it were false, he would be shot. But if he were shot, the statement would have been true. So there is a contradiction, and his statement was neither true nor false. They couldn't shoot him or hang him. So they let him free. Actually what happened was that they shot him anyway.

200. (c) 11

Houses that have fewer than six rooms is 10 (given). Houses that have six, seven, or eight rooms is x (unknown). Houses that have more than eight rooms is 4 (given). The total is 25. $10 + x + 4$ must equal 25, so x must be 11.

201. 1. *train* or *drain*
    2. *craft* or *draft*
    3. *stone*
    4. *write*
    5. *blame* or *flame*
    6. *stall*
    7. *phone*
    8. *troll*

9. *place*

10. *grace*

11. *crush*

12. *crave*

13. *swine*

14. *swarm*

15. *scold*

16. *scorn*

17. *scone*

18. *sworn*

19. *spark*

20. *plate*

There are also many more, including sword, spear, stream, spool, etc.

202. They are all exactly divisible by the product of their digits. For example, take 112. 1 × 1 × 2 = 2 and 112/2 = 56.

203. In order for the horse to move, the horse pushes back on the ground. This makes the ground push back on the horse (this is actually Newton's third law). Thus, there is a force exerted by the ground on the horse, which enables the horse to move with the cart.

204.

That is, 4 to the fourth power to the fourth power to the fourth power—quite a huge number.

205. (e) 400

So you don't have to rack your brain in a verbal math problem, always translate "what" to x, "percent" to /100, "of" to × (times), and "is" to =. In the problem above, you would get:

What percent of 5 is 20?

$$\downarrow \quad\quad \downarrow \quad\quad \downarrow\;\downarrow\;\downarrow$$

$$x\;/\;100 \quad \times\;5 = 20$$

This becomes: $(x/100) \times 5 = 20$.

Now here's another strategy. Get rid of the fractions! Multiply both sides of the equation above by 100. You get:

$$\frac{(x)(5)\;\cancel{100}}{\cancel{100}} = 20 \times 100$$

and you find

$(x)(5) = 20 \times 100 = 2,000$; Divide both sides of the equation by 5: $x = 400$.

206. 5″

Draw extra lines to get more information. Draw the radius. The radius of the circle is the same as the diagonal of the rectangle!

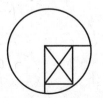

207. First weighing: four against four

Second weighing: two against two

Third weighing: one against one

Try to find a set of balls as "reference" balls, none of which is the heavy or light ball.

Note that even though the scale may tip downward in one direction, the heavy ball may not be on the "downward" part of the scale; it may be that the lighter ball is on the upward side.

Let's work through the solution:

Identify balls by number 1, 2, 3, 4, 5, 6, 7, 8, 9, 10, 11, 12

(1, 2, 3) ? (4, 5, 6) means you weigh 1, 2, 3 vs. 4, 5, 6

If the result of weighing is (1, 2, 3) < (4, 5, 6), it means first group (1, 2, 3) is lighter than the second, (4, 5, 6).

(1, 2, 3) > (4, 5, 6) means the first group (1, 2, 3) is heavier. (1, 2, 3) = (4, 5, 6) means both groups (1, 2, 3) and (4, 5, 6) weigh the same and so all the balls in that group are normal. N represents a normal ball.

Divide 12 balls into 3 groups: (1, 2, 3, 4), (5, 6, 7, 8), (9, 10, 11, 12).

First weighing: weigh (1, 2, 3, 4) ? (5, 6, 7, 8)

CASE 1: Where (1, 2, 3, 4) = (5, 6, 7, 8)

This means that the odd ball is in (9, 10, 11, 12) and that 1, 2, 3, 4, 5, 6, 7, 8 are normal (N)

Second weighing: weigh $(N, 9)$? $(10, 11)$

If $(N, 9) = (10, 11)$

This means the odd ball is 12.

Third weighing: weigh (12) ? (N).

If $(12) > (N)$ then 12 is the heavy ball. If $(12) < (N)$, then 12 is the light ball.

If in the second weighing, $(N, 9) > (10, 11)$, then either 9 is heavy or 10 or 11 is light.

Third weighing: weigh (10) ? (11).

If $(10) > (11)$, then 11 is light and 9 is normal. If $(10) < (11)$, then 10 is light.

If in weighing (10) ? (11), $(10) = (11)$, then 9 must be heavy.

If in the second weighing, $(N, 9) < (10, 11)$, you can similarly reason that 9 is light or 10 or 11 is heavy.

And then in the third weighing, weigh (10) ? (11).

If $(10) > (11)$, then 10 is heavy. If $(10) < (11)$, then 11 is heavy. If $(10) = (11)$, then 9 is light.

CASE 2: Where in the first weighing, $(1, 2, 3, 4) > (5, 6, 7, 8)$.

Then you know that 9, 10, 11, 12 are normal (N), and one of the balls 1, 2, 3, 4 is heavy or one of the balls 5, 6, 7, 8 is light.

Second weighing: weigh $(N, 1, 2)$? $(3, 4, 5)$

If $(N, 1, 2) = (3, 4, 5)$ then the odd ball is in $(6, 7, 8)$ and is lighter, so weigh (6) ? (7) and pick the lightest. If (6) = (7) then 8 is light.

If $(N, 1, 2) > (3, 4, 5)$, (3, 4) are normal, so odd is in (1, 2, 5).

Third weighing: weigh (1) ? (2).

If (1) > (2) then 1 is heavy; if (1) < (2), then 2 is heavy; if (1) = (2), then 5 is light.

Second weighing: For the case where $(N, 1, 2) < (3, 4, 5)$, the odd ball is in (3, 4) and is heavy, since 5 can't be heavy, and (1, 2), which were in the heavy group originally, are not the heavy ones, now.

Third weighing: So weigh (3) ? (4). If (3) > (4), 3 is heavy. If (3) < (4), then 4 is heavy.

CASE 3: Where in the first weighing, $(1, 2, 3, 4) < (5, 6, 7, 8)$.

Second weighing: weigh $(N, 1, 2)$? (3, 4, 5). If $(N, 1, 2) = (3, 4, 5)$, odd ball is in (6, 7, 8) and is heavier, so weigh (6) ? (7) (third weighing) and pick the heaviest. If (6) = (7), then 8 is heavy.

If $(N, 1, 2) > (3, 4, 5)$, the odd ball is in (3, 4) and is light, since according to the first weighing, (5) can't be light and (1, 2) cannot be heavy.

Third weighing: So weigh (3) ? (4). If (3) > (4), then 4 is light. If (3) < (4), then 3 is light.

If in the second weighing, $(N, 1, 2) < (3, 4, 5)$, then either

(1,2) is light or 5 is heavy because of the first weighing.

Third weighing: So weigh (1) ? (2). If (1) > (2), then 2 is light. If (1) < (2), then 1 is light. If (1) = (2), then 5 is heavy.

208. (b) The third student's hat can be white.

Think of what information you get by knowing that both the first and second students cannot figure out the color of their hats.

The color of the third student's hat is red. He reasons, "If I can prove it's impossible that I have a white hat, then I must have a red hat." There are only three scenarios in which the last student could have a white hat:

(1) if the first student has a red hat and the second student has a white hat,

(2) if the first student has a white hat and the second student has a red hat, and

(3) if both the first and second students have red hats.

Scenario (1) is ruled out because the first student would have known his hat was red if the other two students had white hats, since there were only two white hats in the original bag. Scenario (2) is ruled out because the second student would have made the same deduction. Scenario (3) is ruled out because the second student would have known she was wearing a red hat if the third student was wearing a white hat, because otherwise the first student would have seen that they were both wearing white hats. But because the second student did not know or figure out that she was wearing a red hat, the third student could not be wearing a white hat. Thus the only combinations are (where A, B, C denote first, second, third student respectively):

A—White; B—White; C—Red

A— White; B—Red; C—Red

A—Red; B—White; C—Red

A—Red; B—Red; C—Red

Thus, (b) is correct.

209. 3 to 4

Translate from words to math. Let S be the ship's age now; B is the boiler's age now; s is the ship's age then; and b is the boiler's age then. You would get:

(1) $S = 2b$

(2) $s = B$

(3) B/S unknown

(4) $B - b = S - s$, because $B - b$ and $S - s$ represents the same passage of time.

Substituting (1) in the left side of (4) and (2) in the right side of (4), we get:

(5) $B - S/2 = S - B$

Thus, we get:

(6) $2B = 3S/2$ or

(7) $B/S = 3/4$

210. 9/20

Call females F1, F2, F3, and call males M1, M2, M3. The total number of combinations of three people, such as F1, F2, M1 and F1, M2, M3, etc., is six combinations taken three at a time, or 6C3, which is equal to $(6 \times 5 \times 4) / (3 \times 2 \times 1) = 20$. The favorable number of combinations is nine:

M1, M2, F1

M1, M2, F2

M1, M2, F3

M1, M3, F1

M1, M3, F2

M1, M3, F3

M2, M3, F1

M2, M3, F2

M2, M3, F3

Thus the probability of only two males in the room is favorable ways / total ways = 9/20.

THE GEOMETRY PROBLEM THAT STUMPED THE NATION
Solution

1. Draw EF parallel to BC. Then angle DFE = 80° because of equal corresponding angles of parallel lines.

2. Drop a perpendicular line to BC from A, hitting BC at G. Because of congruent triangles ABG and AGC, angle BAG = angle CAG = 10°.

3. Now draw line FC, calling H the point where line FC intersects line BE. Line AG passes through point H, because of symmetry.

4. Angle BHC = 60° since the other angles of the triangle BHC are both 60°.

5. BE = FC (because of corresponding sides of congruent triangles FBC and EBC). BH = HC (call BH *b*) because triangle BHC is isosceles. So by subtraction, FH = HE.

6. Since angle FHE = 60° (vertical angle to BHC), and because FH = HE from 5, angle FHE = angle HEF = 60°, so triangle FHE is equilateral. Thus, FE = FH = HE. Call each of those sides *a*.

7. Now AF = AE (because AB = AC and FB = EC, by subtraction AF = AE).

8. Because triangle AEB is isosceles, AE = BE = *b* + *a*. Thus, AF = BE = *b* + *a* (since AF = AE from 7).

9. BE = FC (congruent triangles BEC and BFC), so AF = FC, since AF = BE from 8.

10. Now watch this: Triangle AFH is congruent to triangle CFD because AF = FC; angle AFH = 140° = angle CFD; angle DCF = 10° = angle FAH. Thus, corresponding sides of the congruent triangles AFH and triangle CFD are equal, so FH = FD. But FH = FE from 6, so FE = FD.

11. Since FE = FD, angle FDE = angle FED and since angle DFE = 80° from (1), angle FDE = 50° = angle FED.

12. But angle FDC = 30°, so by subtraction, angle EDC = 20°!

ABOUT THE AUTHOR

Gary R. Gruber, PhD, is recognized nationally as the leading expert on standardized tests and originator and developer of the critical-thinking skills necessary for use on standardized tests. It is said that no one in the nation is better at assessing the thinking patterns of how a person answers questions and providing the mechanism to improve the faulty thinking approaches. Dr. Gruber's SAT score improvements with students have been documented to be the highest in the nation.

Dr. Gruber's unique methods have been used by the Public Broadcasting Service (PBS), Sylvan Learning Centers, and *Grolier's Encyclopedia*, and they are being used by school districts throughout the country, in homes and workplaces across the nation, and by a host of other entities. Most recently he has trained the University of California's teachers to create programs for specific critical-thinking and problem-solving skills for their minority programs.

Dr. Gruber holds a doctorate in physics and has published more than thirty-five books with major publishers on test-taking and critical-thinking methods, with over seven million copies sold. He has also authored over one thousand articles in both scholarly journals as well as in newspapers syndicated nationally, has appeared on numerous television and radio shows, and has been interviewed in hundreds of publications. He has developed major programs for school districts and for city and state educational agencies for improving and restructuring curriculum, increasing learning ability and test scores, increasing motivation, developing a passion for learning and problem solving, and decreasing student dropout rates. His results have been lauded throughout the country by people from all walks of life.

His mission is to get the nation impassioned with learning and problem solving so that people don't merely try to get a quick answer, but actually enjoy and look forward to solving the problem and learning. With this approach, Dr. Gruber believes that we'd have a nation of critical thinkers who would find problem solving enjoyable. Because of Dr. Gruber's tenacity, passion, and creativity for solving problems, and having used the strategies he has developed and honed for years, the *Washington Post* has called him "the super genius."